SYLV

THE AMERICAN WAY

LoNN

Course software

↓

MEI (TUTOR)

* scratch food * convenience/prepared food

* save for rainy days

THE AMERICAN WAY

An Introduction to American Culture

Edward N. Kearny *Western Kentucky University*
Mary Ann Kearny *Kentucky English Language Institute*
Jo Ann Crandall *Center for Applied Linguistics*

Prentice Hall Regents, Englewood Cliffs, NJ 07632

Library of Congress Cataloging in Publication Data

KEARNY, EDWARD N. (DATE)
The American Way.

Includes bibliographies.
1. English language—Text-books for foreign speakers.
2. Readers—United States. I. Kearny, Mary Ann.
II. Crandall, Jo Ann. III. Title.
PE1128.K39 1984 428.6'4 83-11042
ISBN 0-13-031682-2

Editorial/production supervision and
interior design: Dan Mausner
Cover design: 20/20 Services, Inc.
Manufacturing buyer: Harry P. Baisley

Printed in the United States of America

20 19 18 17 16 15 14 13

ISBN 0-13-031682-2

PRENTICE-HALL INTERNATIONAL, INC., *London*
PRENTICE-HALL OF AUSTRALIA PTY. LIMITED, *Sydney*
EDITORA PRENTICE-HALL DO BRASIL, LTDA., *Rio de Janeiro*
PRENTICE-HALL CANADA INC., *Toronto*
PRENTICE-HALL OF INDIA PRIVATE LIMITED, *New Delhi*
PRENTICE-HALL OF JAPAN, INC., *Tokyo*
PRENTICE-HALL OF SOUTHEAST ASIA PTE. LTD., *Singapore*
WHITEHALL BOOKS LIMITED, *Wellington, New Zealand*

Contents

Dedicated to Lisa Kearny, Joseph Keyerleber,
and our friends at the Center for Applied Linguistics

Preface

Why a book on American culture? There are many reasons. Those of us who have worked with foreign students in American universities or who have taught English to students both there and overseas are repeatedly confronted by questions about life in the United States. Students who are preparing to come to the United States to study or who are already enrolled in English as a Second Language or other programs in American universities frequently are confused or even mystified about the values, attitudes, and cultural patterns that surround them. Even those students who have mastered enough English to take courses in an American university may find that they have not adequately mastered the cultural rules that are required for them to be successful American students. Many of these rules can be understood only within the broader context of American cultural patterns in general.

It is not only students who need information of the kind presented here. Foreign businesspeople, visiting scholars or government officials, and even tourists would find their time spent in the United States more satisfying if they were able to understand more of the values underlying American behavior patterns and institutions. Newly arrived immigrants or refugees, as well, would find adaptation to their new home easier if they had a systematic introduction to their new country and its inhabitants.

Thus, *The American Way* is suitable for a variety of students. It has been used as a text in a number of programs for foreign students, including short summer courses in the United States for foreign high school and college students, both quarter and semester courses at American universities, and government courses for foreign visitors and immigrants. Interestingly, an American Culture and Society course taught by one of the authors also had American students enrolled, and they perhaps learned as much as the foreign students during the semester.

What do we really learn when we study about other cultures? First and foremost, we learn about our own, for until we are confronted by a different way of doing things, we assume that everyone does things the same way that we do, and thus our own culture—our values, attitudes, behavior—are largely hidden from our view. When we spend some time analyzing another culture, however, we begin to see our own more clearly and to understand some of the subtleties that motivate our behavior and our opinions. Thus, students using this book cannot help but begin to understand themselves and their own cultures better as a result. To enhance this understanding, we have followed each of the chapters with a series of exercises, some of them specifically designed to encourage students to think about their own values or patterns of behavior and to compare these with what they are learning about or experiencing in American settings. We have also included a number of exercises that are intended subtly to "force" foreign students to interact with and talk with Americans. In these exercises we have provided a set of carefully structured questions which can be asked to a number of Americans, in order for the student to get a composite picture of American beliefs and practices as they relate to education, business, government, sports, recreation, and so on. If your students cannot find an American to ask, then reference works can be consulted for answers (some of these reference works are indicated in the questions), or if the student has access to American television programs or movies, careful observation and analysis will yield interesting answers as well.

A number of exercises are also provided that improve study skills, writing skills, or reading skills, and thus help the student become more effective in an American university. We believe that students need experience presenting information and their own personal opinions to others, and they should be encouraged to make reports to the class and participate in debates and formal discussions. Outlining exercises provide instruction in how to organize information into main ideas and supporting details.

Some of the chapter exercises will provide students with an opportunity to explore more fully an idea that has been presented or to discuss these ideas with other students. You may wish to assign different exercises to different students or small groups of students and then ask them to share their findings and opinions with the rest of the class. If possible, small groups should include students from different countries so that in addition to learning about American culture and their own, they are also learning about others.

Perhaps this is the real goal of a culture course: to help us become more sensitive to cultural differences and more accepting of them. However, there will always be things about another culture that we do not "like," no matter how much we might understand it. Thus, the objective of this book is not to persuade others to approve of all facets of life in the United States, but rather to help them understand it more fully and be able to adapt, even if only temporarily, whenever it is desirable to do so. There are always opportunities for exploiting one's "foreignness," but there are also times when being from a different culture can be a real liability. The ultimate choice is up to the individual, but we hope that this introduction and cultural overview will enable people working or studying with Americans to make more informed choices.

The Book at a Glance

Purpose: To increase students' awareness and understanding of the cultural values of the United States, their own country, and, it is hoped, other countries.

To help strengthen the study skills of ESL students who plan to attend academic institutions in the United States.

Level: High intermediate to advanced. The vocabulary level is in the range of 2,500 to 3,000 words. Grammatical structures are not controlled, although an effort has been made to avoid overly complex patterns.

Content: Information about basic American values and how these values affect various institutions and aspects of life in the United States: religion, business, government, race relations, education, recreation, and the family.

Types of Exercises: Vocabulary practice, comprehension check, questions for discussion and composition, cloze summary paragraph, outlining, skimming, values clarification, questions for Americans, suggestions for research, suggestions for writing, debate topics, proverbs, people watching, understanding the media, suggestions for further reading, experiments.

Use of Text: In ESL classes to teach
- —reading skills
- —composition
- —conversation
- —study skills

In culture classes (or ESL classes) for
- —cultural orientation
- —cross-cultural communication

Acknowledgments

We wish to acknowledge the assistance and encouragement we received from C.W. Twyford and Ellen Comer, both of whom read the manuscript, made helpful suggestions, and field-tested the materials in their respective programs. We would also like to thank the numbers of foreign students we have worked with over the years for sharing their insights and perceptions of the United States with us, and in the process, for helping us to better understand our own American culture.

E.N.K.
M.A.K.
J.A.C.

Memorial Day in Salisbury, Connecticut. *UN PHOTO by F. B. Grunzweig.*

chapter 1

Introduction

Culture hides much more than it reveals, and strangely enough what it hides, it hides most effectively from its own participants. Years of study have convinced me that the real job is not to understand foreign culture but to understand our own.

Edward T. Hall

Recently a British gentleman who was visiting the United States said, "I don't think it's possible to write a book about the American character. The United States is too large; the people and their **lifestyles** are too different. The country is changing too rapidly, and the future is so uncertain."

Perhaps he is right. It may be impossible to describe the average American. For that matter, it may not be possible to describe the typical Japanese, or Swede, or Brazilian, or Nigerian. However, possible or not, people are naturally curious about each other, and when they meet people from different countries, they want to know about them:

- What life is like in their country
- What kind of houses they live in
- What kind of food they eat
- What their customs are

If we visit their country, we can observe the people and how they live, and we can answer some of these questions. But the most interesting questions are often the hardest to answer.

- What do the people believe in?
- What do they value most in life?
- What **motivates** them?
- Why do they behave the way they do?

In trying to answer these questions about Americans, we must remember two things: (1) the immense size of the United States; and (2) its enormous **ethnic diversity**. It is difficult to comprehend the size of the country until you have tried to travel from one city to another. If you got in a car in New York and drove to Los Angeles, stopping only to get gas, eat, and sleep, it would take you four or five days. It takes two full days to drive from New York to Florida. On a typical day in November the national **weather forecast** might call for rain in New York and snow in Chicago, while it was warm enough to swim in Los Angeles. It is not difficult to imagine how different daily life might be in such different climates, or how lifestyles could vary in cities and towns so far apart.

There is a second important **factor** influencing American life: ethnic diversity. Aside from the native American Indians who were living on the North

Marc Anderson.

Joseph Keyerleber.

American continent when the first European settlers arrived, all Americans came from foreign countries—or their ancestors did. In some cases, Americans feel very strongly about their ethnic **heritage**. For example, in parts of Minnesota and Wisconsin some people still refer to each other as "Swedes" or "Danes" or "Norwegians," even though their ancestors left their home countries and settled in the United States a hundred years ago. Even Americans with little knowledge of what countries their ancestors came from, and little sense of having a particular ethnic heritage, may carry on a family tradition without realizing what the origin of the tradition is. For example, one family may traditionally open Christmas presents on Christmas Eve while another always waits until Christmas morning. Neither family may realize that they are honoring a tradition brought to the United States from another country by a long-forgotten ancestor.

In spite of these very important differences, however, a strong tie binds Americans together. That tie is a sense of national identity—of "being an American." Incidentally, when citizens of the United States refer to themselves as "Americans," they have no intention of excluding people from Latin American countries. There is no word such as "United Statesians" in the English language, so people call themselves Americans. Thus, what is really a language problem has sometimes caused misunderstandings. Although citizens of Latin American countries may call the people in the United States "North Americans," to people in the United States this makes no sense at all, because the term "North American" refers to Canadians as well as citizens of the United States. (The word

American Indian Tribesmen, c. 1913. *Rodman Wanamaker.*

"American," then, will be used in this text as the adjective and nationality for the people who live in the United States of America.)

What, then, can we say about these Americans? What holds them together and makes them feel "American"? Is it possible to make **generalizations** about what they believe? It is, but we must be cautious about generalizations. As we talk about basic American beliefs, we must remember that not all Americans hold these beliefs, nor do all Americans believe these things to the same degree. In fact, a minority will disagree strongly with some of these beliefs. The way in which some Americans carry out their beliefs may also differ, resulting in a great variety of lifestyles. However, even in these lifestyles we will find some patterns.

Throughout this book we will be drawing on the wisdom of a famous observer of the American scene, Alexis de Tocqueville. Tocqueville came to the United States as a young Frenchman in 1831 to study the American form of democracy and what it might mean to the rest of the world. After a visit of only nine months he wrote a **remarkable** book called *Democracy in America,* which is a "classic study of the American way of life." Tocqueville had remarkable powers of observation. He described not only the democratic system of government and how it operated, but also its effect on how Americans think, feel, and act. Many **scholars** believe that he had a deeper understanding of basic American beliefs and values than anyone else who has ever written about the United States. What is so remarkable is that many of the **traits** of the American character which he observed over 150 years ago are still visible and meaningful today.

Pioneer life in 1882. *Library of Congress.*

Another reason why Tocqueville's observations of the American character are important is the time when he visited the United States. He came in the 1830s, before America was industrialized. This was the **era** of the small farmer, the small businessman, and the settling of the western frontier. Americans look back at this period as the golden age of the **pioneers**. In hard times they speak of the moral character of the pioneers and they remember their frontier heritage with pride. To them, this era represents the best of the American character. The qualities and character traits Tocqueville describes are the same ones that Americans take pride in today. He, however, was a **neutral** observer and saw both the good and the bad sides of these qualities.

This is a book about those basic American beliefs, values, and character traits. It is not a book of cold facts about American behavior or institutions, but rather it is about the motivating forces behind the people and their institutions. It is about how these basic beliefs and values affect important **facets** of American life: religion, business, work and play, politics, the family, and education.

We invite you to participate in this book. We will describe what most Americans think and believe, but you will have an opportunity to test these descriptions by making your own observations. As you read about these basic values, think of them as working hypotheses which you can test on Americans, on people of other nations, and on people of your nationality. Compare them with your own values and beliefs and with what is most important in your life. Through this process, you should emerge with a better understanding not only of

Americans, but also of your own culture and yourself. It is by studying others that we learn about ourselves.

New Words

lifestyle the way people live: their clothes, their homes, their jobs, their leisure activities
motivate to cause someone to do something or act in a certain way (a motive is an idea or feeling which causes someone to act)
ethnic diversity having people of many different races and nationalities
weather forecast the news of what the weather will be that day
factor point; ideas or elements that cause a result
heritage something that comes to us from the past
generalization a statement that is generally true
remarkable surprisingly good
scholar someone who studies a subject thoroughly
trait characteristic
era time, period of time
pioneers the first settlers of the West; people who are the first to do something new
neutral not taking one side or the other; seeing both sides (the good and the bad)
facet element; part; side

A. Vocabulary Exercise

Supply the word or phrase from the vocabulary list which correctly completes the sentence.

1. If you want to know if it will rain today, turn on the radio or TV and listen to the w________ f________
2. People who are the first to do something new, such as the first people who settled in the West, are called p________.
3. If you want to discuss the characteristics of someone's personality, you can speak of that person's personality t________.
4. Something that is surprisingly good is r________.
5. If two countries are at war and a third country chooses not to take sides, the third country may declare itself n________.
6. The history of a country—the historical events and the traditions—everything which comes from the past makes up its h________.
7. Someone who lives and works on a farm has a different l________ from someone who lives in the city and works in an office.

8. Unlike some other countries which do not have people of many different races and nationalities, the United States has great ethnic diversity
9. If I state something that is generally true—such as, "Most Americans are proud of their freedom"—I am making a generalization .
10. If we want to understand why people think and act the way they do, we must understand what motivate them.
11. A person who has studied a subject thoroughly, such as a "historian" who has studied history, is called a scholar
12. The human personality is not simple; it has many elements or facets .
13. For a period of time in the 1930s and 1940s big bands were very popular in the United States. It was the big band era .
14. If the economy of a country suddenly improves, there may be many reasons or factors which have caused the change.

B. Comprehension Check

Write T if the statement is true and F if it is false according to the information in the chapter.

T 1. Because of the great size of the United States, there are many different climates.

F 2. All people in the United States have the same lifestyle.

F 3. All people living in the United States today came from another country, or their ancestors did.

F 4. Americans do not know or care what country their ancestors came from.

F 5. Americans have long forgotten the customs brought to the United States by their ancestors.

T 6. Although Americans may be very different, there is still a strong feeling of what it means to be an American.

T 7. The English language has no adjective for "United States" and therefore uses the term "American" to refer to its people.

F 8. It is not possible to make generalizations about what Americans believe because they are so different.

T 9. Many of the characteristics of Americans which Alexis de Tocqueville observed 150 years ago are still true today.

T 10. Many Americans think of the time when Tocqueville came (1830s) as a time when Americans were at their best.

C. Questions for Discussion and Composition

1. What effect does the geography of a country have on its people? Does your country have different climates? What effect does climate have on the lifestyles of the people in your country? How is life in a small country different from life in a large one?
2. What different ethnic groups are there in your country? Where do they live? How are they different from the majority of people in your country: language? clothing? food? music? customs? What effect do different ethnic groups have on a country?
3. Who was Alexis de Tocqueville? When did he visit the United States? What was the country like then? Why is his book still studied today?
4. Do you think it is possible to describe the average person in your country and what he or she believes? How would you describe the traits of the people in your country? Do you think people all over the world are basically the same or basically very different? How are Americans different from people in your country?

D. Cloze Summary Paragraph

This paragraph summarizes the chapter. Fill in each blank with any word which makes sense.

In describing the beliefs ____*of*____ the average American, it __________ important to consider the __________ size of the United __________ and its enormous ethnic __________. Except for the native __________ Indians, all Americans, or __________ ancestors, came from another __________. Some Americans are very __________ of their ethnic origins __________ others are not. In __________ of their many differences, __________ have a sense of __________ identity. They share many __________ beliefs although they may __________ different lifestyles. In the __________ a Frenchman named Tocqueville __________ American life and basic __________. Many of his observations

__________ still true today. Americans __________ that the qualities of __________ American pioneers of the __________ represent the best of __________ American character.

E. Ask Americans

Interview at least three Americans of different ages (one under 21, one middle-aged and one over 60) and ask them to complete the following questions.

1. Americans are __________.
2. They like __________.
3. They don't really __________.
4. Most Americans feel __________.
5. They act __________.
6. Most Americans believe in __________.
7. The United States is a country where __________.
8. The average American is __________.
9. Americans today are worried about __________.
10. The most important thing in life to most Americans is __________.

F. Ask Yourself

What do you think Americans are like? Mark the following chart to show which characteristics Americans have compared with people in your country. The closer to the word you put your X, the stronger your feeling that this word describes Americans.

tall _X_ ___ ___ ___ ___ short

This answer would show that you think Americans are much taller than people in your country.

tall ___ ___ _X_ ___ ___ short

This answer would show that you think they are about the same—neither taller, nor shorter.

tall ___ ___ ___ _X_ ___ short

This answer would show that you think Americans are a little shorter than people in your country.

1. friendly ___ ___ ___ ___ ___ unfriendly
2. unhappy ___ ___ ___ ___ ___ happy
3. helpful ___ ___ ___ ___ ___ not helpful
4. shy ___ ___ ___ ___ ___ outgoing

5. thin	___	___	___	___	___	fat
6. poor	___	___	___	___	___	rich
7. quiet	___	___	___	___	___	loud
8. cooperative	___	___	___	___	___	competitive
9. active	___	___	___	___	___	passive
10. lazy	___	___	___	___	___	hard-working
11. well-dressed	___	___	___	___	___	poorly-dressed
12. dirty	___	___	___	___	___	clean
13. positive	___	___	___	___	___	negative
14. hostile	___	___	___	___	___	loving
15. satisfied	___	___	___	___	___	dissatisfied
16. attractive	___	___	___	___	___	unattractive
17. aggressive	___	___	___	___	___	not aggressive
18. loyal	___	___	___	___	___	disloyal
19. selfish	___	___	___	___	___	concerned for others
20. patient	___	___	___	___	___	impatient

Decide whether each characteristic listed above is positive or negative. If it is positive, give a score of +1 or +2. If it is negative, give a score of −1 or −2. If you mark the center blank, count the pair as 0.

	+2	+1	0	−1	−2	
positive	___	___	___	___	___	negative
	−2	−1	0	+1	+2	
negative	___	___	___	___	___	positive

Add up the scores for each pair and compare scores with those of other students in the class.

G. People Watching

Different countries have different rules for personal space—that is, when people touch, how close they stand when they are speaking to one another, how close strangers sit, how people behave on elevators, etc. People are usually not consciously aware of these rules, but they become very uncomfortable if the rules are broken and "their space" is entered without permission. You can discover the rules by observing people interacting and also by testing or breaking the rules to see how other people respond.

Perform the experiments below and record in a journal the reactions of the people involved. Use your journal to record other observations you make while "people watching." It may be helpful to work in pairs, with one person testing the rule while the other observes and records what happens. If you are not in the United States and if you do not have an opportunity to observe Americans, you may still conduct these experiments on people from your own country.

Rule: Americans have a bubble of space around their bodies which is about an inch thick. This bubble of space must not be broken by a stranger. If American strangers touch each other accidentally, they mutter an apology such as "Pardon me," "Excuse me," "Oh, I'm sorry," or just "Sorry."

Observation: Watch people in a crowd, standing in line, waiting as a group, or passing on a street or in a hallway. Who is touching whom? What does their relationship appear to be? What happens when people touch accidentally? How does the person touched respond? What does the one who has broken the other's bubble do? Record gestures, facial expressions, emotional responses, and words exchanged.

Experiment: See how close you can stand to someone in a crowd without touching him or her. Try breaking someone's bubble of space with a very light touch of your elbow or arm. What is the person's response? Try leaning against a person very gently. What happens? (*Warning*: This may provoke an angry response!)

Rule: When standing in elevators, Americans usually face the door, speak quietly, and try to avoid touching one another. If a stranger enters an elevator where there is only one other person, he or she will stand on the opposite side of the elevator. As more people get on the elevator, they occupy the corners first and then try to disperse themselves evenly throughout the available space.

Bill Jackson.

Observation: Observe people in elevators. Which direction are they facing? If you are alone in an elevator and someone comes in, where does he or she stand? As more people enter the elevator, where do they stand? Do the people talk to one another? How loudly do they speak? Do strangers touch? What happens in a crowded elevator when someone in the back has to get off?

Experiment: Get on an elevator where there is only one person and stand next to him or her. What is the person's reaction? In an elevator where there are a number of people, turn and face the group with your back to the door. How do the people react? Have a conversation with someone in a crowded elevator and don't lower your voice. How do you think the people feel about this? Note their facial expressions.

H. Understanding Polls

In the United States conducting opinion polls is very popular. A newspaper, a magazine, a TV station, or a professional polling organization asks a representative group of Americans several questions to determine what their opinions are about a given topic. The people chosen for the poll are supposed to represent a broad cross-section of the American population. That is, the pollsters choose men and women of different ages, occupations, and races in the same proportion that these groups are found in the population. Sometimes, however, a random sample is taken which picks people by chance. Both methods are designed to learn what the average person, sometimes called "the man in the street," believes.

Polls are very popular around election time because everyone wants to know which candidate is ahead in the race and what the voters are thinking about the key issues of the campaign. Many politicians have their own polling organizations to keep them in constant touch with public opinion. There are three well-known polling organizations which measure public opinion on a variety of topics: Louis Harris and Associates, the Roper Organization, and Gallup International Research Institutes. A poll conducted by these groups is popularly referred to as "a Harris poll," "a Roper poll," or "a Gallup poll." Results of different polling organizations on diverse topics may be found in a magazine called *Public Opinion.**

In the polls on page 13, people in several different countries were asked how satisfied or dissatisfied they were with their lives. Study the two polls and then answer these questions.

1. Which group conducted these polls—Harris, Roper, or Gallup?
2. What year were these polls taken?
3. How did the people answering these questions indicate how satisfied or dissatisfied they were with their lives? What words or numbers did they use when they gave their answers?

* *Public Opinion,* sold by subscription only, is published bimonthly by the American Enterprise Institute for Public Policy Research, 1150 Seventeenth Street, N.W., Washington, D.C. 20036.

4. In the first poll, the responses to five questions are shown. How many are shown in the second poll?
5. In the first poll, which country has the largest percentage of people who are satisfied with the way democracy is working in their country?
6. Which two countries have almost the same percentage of people who are satisfied with their standard of living?
7. In the second poll, which country has the least number of people who are satisfied with life as a whole?

IS THE GRASS GREENER HERE?

Question: Now, here are some questions concerning how satisfied—or dissatisfied—you are with various things about your life, such as your standard of living, your education, and so on. To indicate this, would you use this card. (Respondents were handed a card with numbers running from 0 to 10.) If you are extremely satisfied with something you would call off the highest number, 10. If you are extremely dissatisfied you would mention the lowest number, 0. If you are neither extremely satisfied nor extremely dissatisfied, you would mention a number in between 0 and 10—the higher the number the more satisfied, the lower the number the more dissatisfied.

Note: The highly satisfied are those who selected levels 8-10. Graph shows responses from Germany, the United States, and France.

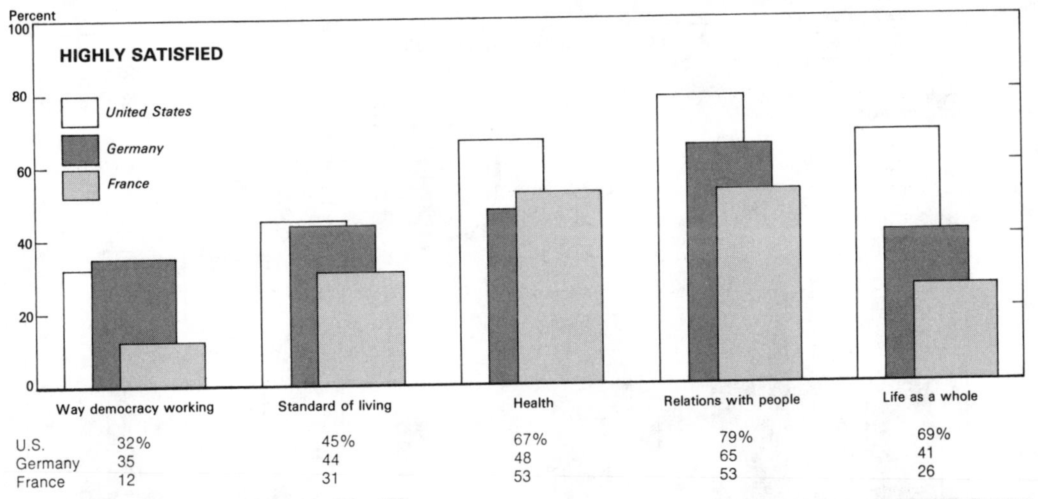

	Way democracy working	Standard of living	Health	Relations with people	Life as a whole
U.S.	32%	45%	67%	79%	69%
Germany	35	44	48	65	41
France	12	31	53	53	26

Source: Survey by Gallup International Research Institutes, 1977.

Public Opinion, July/August 1978

TAKING NATIONAL TEMPERATURES

Question: (Same as in "Is the Grass Greener Here?", with responses to "life as a whole.")

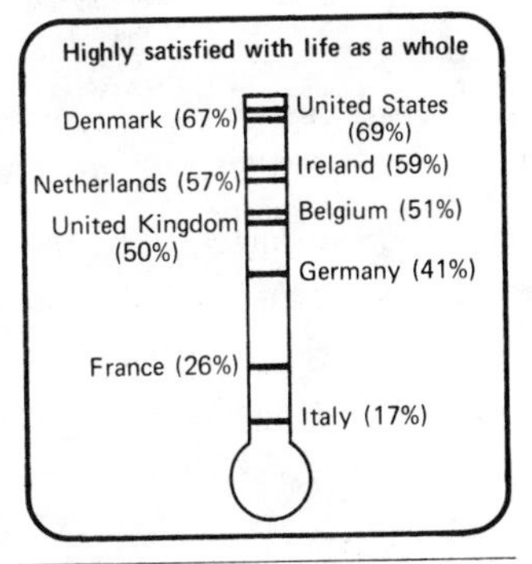

Note: The highly satisfied are those who selected levels 8-10.
Source: Survey by Gallup International Research Institutes, 1977.

I. Suggestions for Writing

It is difficult to make generalizations about what Americans believe because the country is so large and there is so much ethnic diversity. The following polls measure liberalism by race, age, sex, religion, and region.

The map of the regions shows which areas of the country are most liberal and which are most conservative. What do the terms "high technology states" and "heartland states" refer to? The thermometer shows the relative liberalism of all the groups. Which religious group is most liberal—Catholics, Protestants, or Jews? Are American women more liberal than men?

Write a paragraph summarizing the results of these polls, or write a comparison/contrast essay comparing the liberalism of people in your country with that of Americans.

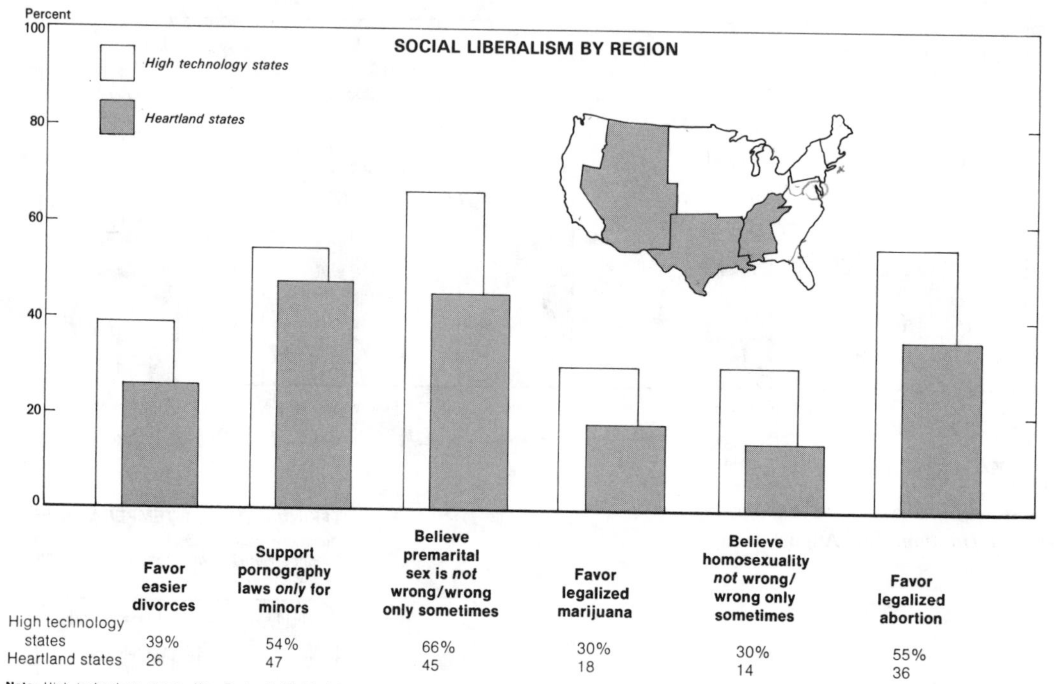

Note: High technology states = New England, Middle Atlantic and Pacific states. Heartland states = East South Central, West South Central, and Mountain states.

Public Opinion, July/August 1978

WHICH GROUP IS *MOST* LIBERAL

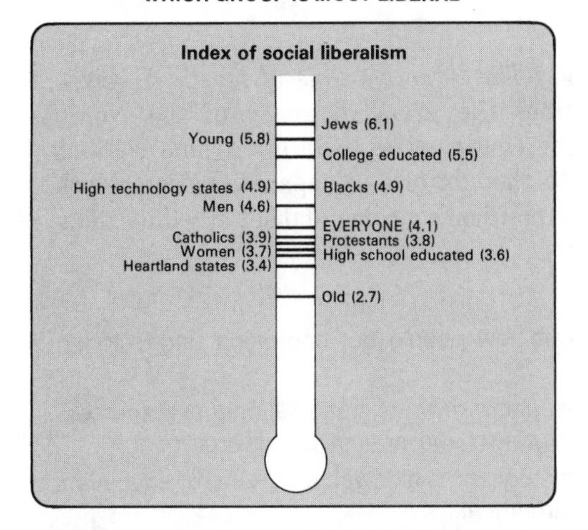

Note: This "social liberalism" measure was created by combining the proportions of the several groups giving "liberal" responses on each of five NORC questions: those on divorce, pornography, premarital sex, marijuana, and abortion. The groups are arranged on a 0 to 10 scale, where 10 is the most liberal score which, in theory, could be attained and 0 is the most conservative. Readers should note that there is nothing absolute or definitive about the social liberalism ranking. Different scores would be arrived at were we to use "social liberalism" questions other than the chosen five. But the *relative positions* of the groups shown along the thermometer would remain unchanged.

Public Opinion, July/August 1978

Questions: Should divorce in this country be easier or more difficult to obtain than it is now? 1974, 1975, 1977 (Graphed response: Easier)

In general, do you favor or oppose the busing of (Negro/Black) and white school children from one school district to another? 1972, 1974, 1975, 1977 (Graphed response: Favor)

Are you in favor of the death penalty for persons convicted of murder? (Question wording in 1972, 1973.) Do you favor or oppose the death penalty for persons convicted of murder? (Question wording in 1974-1977.) 1972-1977 (Graphed response: Oppose)

Which of these statements comes closest to your feelings about pornography laws? There should be laws against the distribution of pornography whatever the age. There should be laws against the distribution of pornography to persons under 18. There should be no laws forbidding the distribution of pornography. 1973, 1975, 1976 (Graphed response: Should be laws for under 18)

There's been a lot of discussion about the way morals and attitudes about sex are changing in this country. If a man and a woman have sex relations before marriage, do you think it is always wrong, almost always wrong, wrong only sometimes, or not wrong at all? 1972, 1974, 1975, 1977 (Graphed response: Wrong only sometimes/Not wrong at all)

Do you think that the use of marijuana should be made legal or not? 1973, 1975, 1976 (Graphed response: Should)

What about sexual relations between two *adults* of the *same* sex—do you think it is always wrong, almost always wrong, wrong only sometimes, or not wrong at all? 1973, 1974, 1976, 1977 (Graphed response: Wrong sometimes/Not at all wrong)

Do you approve or disapprove of a married woman earning money in business or industry if she has a husband capable of supporting her? 1972, 1974, 1975, 1977 (Graphed response: Approve)

Please tell me whether or not you think it should be possible for a pregnant woman to obtain a *legal* abortion . . . if she is married and does not want any more children? 1972-1977 (Graphed response: Yes)

Note: The graphed responses were computed by combining all data from the years in which the questions were asked (dates shown after each question above).

Source: Surveys by National Opinion Research Center, General Social Surveys, 1972-1977.

J. Preparing a Report

Jack Garreau has written a book entitled *The Nine Nations of North America* (Houghton Mifflin) in which he describes the great diversity of the North American continent. He believes that the continent is made up of nine regions which are so different that each might be thought of as a separate nation. Each "nation" has a different culture, economy, political concern, and set of values. The map on page 15 shows the nine nations:

The Empty Quarter: a vast, dry region with few people but enormous undeveloped natural resources.

Ecotopia: an area with high technology jobs, plenty of water, beautiful natural resources, and people with a strong desire to limit growth and protect the environment.

New England: the region with the longest history and a high value on culture, education, high technology, and protecting the environment.

The Foundry: the industrial Northeast, a region of large cities and factories now growing old and losing power and population.

Dixie: the southern region, now experiencing great economic growth, recent industrialization, and enormous social change.

The Islands: southern Florida and the Caribbean, where there is much trade, immigration, and tourism.

MexAmerica: a region growing in power, influence, and money; the center of gas and oil; and the major concentration of Spanish-speaking people.

The Breadbasket: the peaceful Great Plains, the heart of America's agriculture, the keeper of America's traditional values.

Quebec: the home of French-speaking Canadians who maintain their French culture and see themselves as separate from the rest of the world.

Prepare a report to be given to the class on the regions of your country. Include some information on geographical features, natural resources, major cities, and special characteristics of each region.

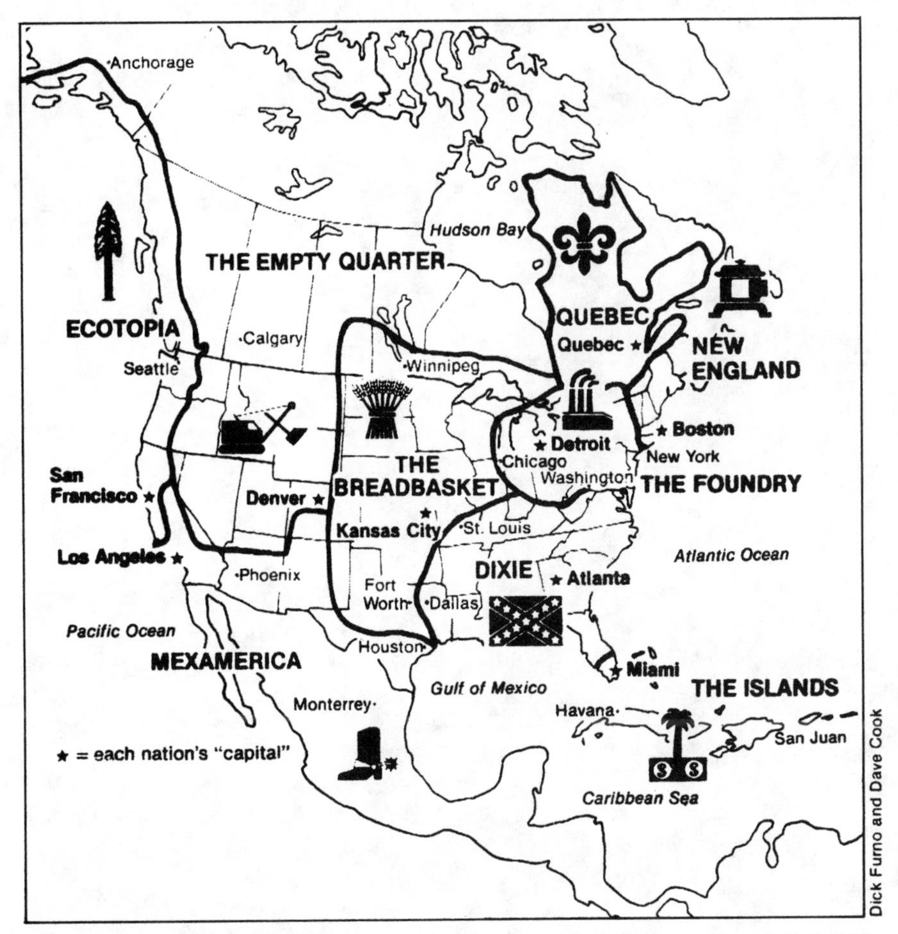

Reprinted from *The Nine Nations of North America* by Joel Garreau. Copyright © 1981 by Joel Garreau. Reprinted by permission of Houghton Mifflin Company.

K. Suggestions for Further Reading

Ralph Waldo Emerson. *Self-Reliance.*
Henry David Thoreau. *Walden.*
Sherwood Anderson. *Winesburg, Ohio.*
Thomas Paine. *The Age of Reason.*
Dee Brown. *Bury My Heart at Wounded Knee.*
O. E. Rölvaag. *Giants in the Earth.*

The March on Washington for Civil Rights, August 28, 1963. *AFL-CIO News.*

chapter 2

Basic American Values and Beliefs

We hold these truths to be self-evident, that all men are created equal, that they are endowed by their Creator with certain inalienable rights, that among these are Life, Liberty and the pursuit of Happiness.

The Declaration of Independence

A refugee who recently arrived in the United States was describing to a group of his fellow musicians what life had been like in his country. He explained that not only the news, but all forms of public communication were censored. There was the tightest security at radio and TV stations, with many armed guards to prevent someone from broadcasting information that had not been approved by the government."Even the typewriters had to be registered," he said, "like a gun." The Americans laughed. "Oh, yes, a typewriter is a powerful weapon. Almost no one has one. They are that difficult to get."

The Americans laughed at the thought of a typewriter as a weapon because in the United States people are free to say and write about almost everything. Freedom is so much a part of American life that it is often taken for granted. But this is not to say that it is not valued. Indeed, the belief in the freedom of the individual is probably the most basic and most strongly held of all American beliefs. (poll, p. 20.) The desire for freedom is what motivated this man to risk his life to come to the United States, and it is one of the main reasons why immigrants have traditionally come to this country.

Individual Freedom and Self-Reliance

The earliest settlers came to the North American continent to establish colonies which were free from the controls that existed in European societies. They wanted to escape the controls placed on their lives by kings and governments, priests and churches, noblemen and aristocrats. To a great extent, they succeeded. In 1776 the British colonial settlers declared their independence from England and established a new nation, the United States of America. In so doing, they **overthrew** the king of England and declared that the power to govern would lie in the hands of the people. They were now free from the power of the kings. In 1789, when they wrote the Constitution for their new nation, they separated church and state so that there would never be a government-supported church. This greatly limited the power of the church. Also, in writing the Constitution they expressly forbade titles of nobility to ensure that an aristocratic society would not develop. There would be no ruling class of noblemen in the new nation.

The historic decisions made by those first settlers have had a **profound** effect on the shaping of the American character. By limiting the power of the government and the churches and **eliminating** a formal aristocracy, they created a climate of freedom where the emphasis was on the individual. The United States came to be associated in their minds with the concept of *individual freedom.* This is probably the most basic of all the American values. Scholars and outside observers often call this value "individualism," but many Americans use the word "freedom." Perhaps the word "freedom" is one of the most respected popular words in the United States today.

By "freedom," Americans mean the desire and the ability of all individuals to control their own destiny without outside interference from the government, a ruling noble class, the church, or any other organized authority. The desire to be

Question: What are you proudest of about America? Just tell me briefly in your own words.

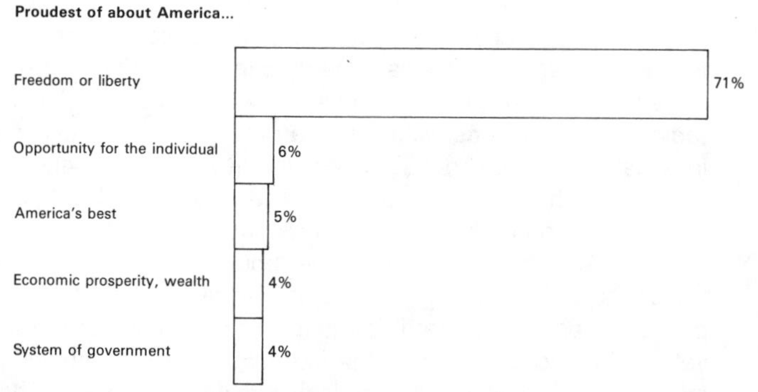

Note: Categories not shown: Science and technology = 1%; military strength = 1%; culture, art = 1%; Other = 6%; None = 1%. The things of which Americans were least proud were Crime = 12%; Iran = 10%; Economic inequality, poverty = 7%; Materialism = 6%; Corruption = 6%. All remaining categories were 5% or less.

Source: Survey by Civic Service, Inc., March 5-18, 1981.

Public Opinion, June/July 1981

free of controls was a basic value of the new nation in 1776, and it has continued to attract immigrants to this country.

There is, however, a price to be paid for this individual freedom: *self-reliance*. Americans believe that individuals must learn to rely on themselves or risk losing freedom. This means achieving both financial and emotional independence from their parents as early as possible, usually by age 18 or 21. It means that Americans believe they should take care of themselves, solve their own problems, and "stand on their own two feet." Tocqueville observed the Americans' belief in self-reliance 150 years ago in the 1830s:

> They owe nothing to any man, they expect nothing from any man; they **acquire** the habit of always considering themselves as standing alone, and they are **apt** to imagine that their whole destiny is in their own hands.

This strong belief in self-reliance continues today as a basic American value. It is perhaps one of the most difficult **aspects** of the American character to understand, but it is profoundly important. Americans believe that they must be self-reliant in order to keep their freedom. If they rely too much on the support of their families or the government or any organization, they may not be free to do what they want.

By being dependent, not only do they risk losing freedom, but they also risk losing the respect of their **peers**. Even if they are not truly self-reliant, most Americans believe they must at least appear to be so. In order to be in the mainstream of American life—to have power and/or respect—individuals must be seen as self-reliant. Although receiving financial support from **charity**, family, or the government is allowed, it is never admired. Many people believe that such individuals are setting a bad example which may weaken the American character as a whole.

Equality of Opportunity and Competition

A second important reason why immigrants have traditionally been drawn to the United States is the belief that everyone has a chance to succeed in the U.S. Generations of immigrants from the earliest settlers to the present day have come with this expectation. They have felt that because individuals are free from excessive political, religious, and social controls, they have a better chance for success. Particularly important is the lack of a **hereditary** aristocracy.

Because titles of nobility were forbidden in the Constitution, no formal class system developed in the United States. In the early years of American history many immigrants chose to leave the older European societies, believing that they had a better chance to succeed in America than in "the old country," where their place in life was determined largely by the social class into which they were born. They knew that in America they would not have to live among noble families who

Immigrants arriving at Ellis Island, New York City. *Library of Congress.*

possessed great power and wealth inherited and accumulated over hundreds of years.

The hopes of many of these immigrants were fulfilled in their new country. The lower social class into which many were born did not prevent them from rising to a higher social position. Many found that they did indeed have a better chance to succeed in the United States than in the old country. Because millions of these immigrants succeeded, Americans came to believe in *equality of opportunity*. When Tocqueville visited the United States in the 1830s, he was impressed by the great uniformity of conditions of life in the new nation. He wrote:

> The more I advanced in the study of American society, the more I perceived that . . . equality of condition is the fundamental fact from which all others seem to be derived.

It is important to understand what Americans mean when they say they believe in equality of opportunity. They do not mean that everyone is—or should be—equal. However, they do mean that each individual should have an equal chance for success. Americans see much of life as a race for success. For them, equality means that everyone should have an equal chance to enter the race and win. In other words, equality of opportunity may be thought of as an ethical rule. It helps ensure that the race for success is a fair one and that a person does not win just because he or she was born into a wealthy family.

President Abraham Lincoln expressed this belief in the 1860s when he said:

> We...wish to allow the humblest man an equal chance to get rich with everybody else. When one starts poor, as most do in the race of life, free society is such that he knows he can better his condition; he knows that there is no fixed condition of labor for his whole life.

There is, however, a price to be paid for this equality of opportunity: *competition.* If much of life is seen as a race, then a person must run the race in order to succeed; a person must compete with others. If every person has an equal chance to succeed in the United States, then it is every person's duty to try. Americans match their energy and intelligence against that of their neighbors in a competitive contest for success. People who like to compete and are more successful than others are honored by being called "winners." On the other hand, those who do not like to compete and are not successful when they try are often dishonored by being called "losers." This is especially true for American men, and it is becoming more and more true for women.

The pressures of competition in the life of an American begin in childhood and continue until retirement from work. Learning to compete successfully is part of growing up in the United States. In a recent opinion poll, 60 percent of the American people agreed with this statement: "It is not healthy for young people to refuse to believe that winning in competition is important." That is, 60 percent believed competition and the desire to win are healthy and desirable. Only 28 percent disagreed.

The pressure to compete causes an American man to be energetic, but it also places a constant emotional strain on him. When he retires at age 65, he is at last free from the pressures of competition. But then a new problem arises. He tends to feel useless and unwanted in a society that gives so much **prestige** to those who compete well. This is one reason why older people in the United States do not have as much honor and respect as they have in other, less competitive societies. In fact, any group of people who do not compete successfully—for whatever reason—do not fit into the mainstream of American life as well as those who do.

Material Wealth and Hard Work

A third reason why immigrants have traditionally come to the United States is to have a better life—that is, to raise their standard of living. For the vast majority of the immigrants who came here, it was probably the most compelling reason for leaving their homeland. Because of its incredibly **abundant** natural resources, the United States appeared to be a "land of plenty" where millions could come to seek their fortunes. Of course, most immigrants did not "get rich overnight," and many of them suffered terribly, but the majority of them were eventually able to improve upon their former standard of living. Even if they were not able to achieve the economic success they wanted, they could be fairly certain that their children would have the opportunity for a better life. The phrase "going from rags to riches" became a **slogan** for the great American dream. Because of the vast riches of the North American continent, the dream came true for many of the immigrants. They achieved material success; they became very attached to material things. *Material wealth* became a value to the American people.

A boatload of Cuban refugees hoping for a better life in the United States. *Official U.S. Coast Guard Photograph.*

Placing a high value on material possessions is called "materialism," but this is a word that most Americans find offensive. To say that a person is "materialistic" is an insult. To an American, this means that this person values material possessions above all else. Americans do not like to be called materialistic because they feel that this unfairly accuses them of loving only material things and of having no religious values. In fact, Americans do have other values and ideals. Nevertheless, acquiring and maintaining a large number of material possessions is of very great importance to most Americans. Why is this so?

Probably the main reason is that material wealth is the most widely accepted measure of social status in the United States. Because Americans rejected the European system of hereditary aristocracy and titles of nobility, they had to find a substitute for judging social status. The quality and quantity of an individual's material possessions became the accepted measure of success and social status. Moreover, as we shall see in later chapters, the American Protestant work ethic associated material success with godliness.

Americans pay a price, however, for their material wealth: *hard work*. The North American continent was rich in natural resources when the first settlers arrived, but all these resources were undeveloped. Only by hard work could these natural resources be converted into material possessions and a comfortable standard of living. Hard work has been both necessary and rewarding for most Americans throughout their history. Because of this, they have come to see material possessions as the natural reward for their hard work. In some ways, material possessions are seen not only as **tangible** evidence of people's work, but also of their abilities. In the late 1700s James Madison, the father of the American Constitution, stated that the difference in material possessions reflected a difference in personal abilities.

More recently, Barry Goldwater, a candidate for the presidency in 1964, said that most poor people are poor because they deserve to be. Most Americans would find this a **harsh** statement, but many might think there was some truth in it. Most Americans believe that if a person works hard, it is possible to have a good standard of living. In a study of teenagers conducted in 1981, researchers found that over 90 percent of young Americans "think they will achieve what they want in life, and almost eight out of ten think they can get what they want through hard work."* There is, however, considerable social pressure not only to maintain a good standard of living but to improve it.

Since people's status in society is frequently measured by how much they own, Americans often feel pressured to buy more than they need. The saying that someone is "keeping up with the Joneses" expresses this urge to buy possessions that are equal to or better than what others have. If Mr. and Mrs. Jones buy a new car, their neighbors may begin to think about buying one too, even if they don't really need a new car. They want to appear as prosperous as everyone else around them, and this means making a continuing effort to buy newer and better material goods.

Automobile Show, New York City.
Marc Anderson.

McCall's, October 1981, p. 47.

In understanding the relationship between what Americans believe and how they live, it is important to distinguish between idealism and reality. American values such as equality of opportunity and self-reliance are ideals that may not necessarily describe the facts of American life. Equality of opportunity, for example, is an ideal that is not always put into practice. In reality, some people have a better chance for success than others. Those who are born into rich families have more opportunities than those who are born into poorer families. Inheriting money does give a person a decided advantage. Many black Americans have fewer opportunities than the average white American, in spite of laws designed to promote equality of opportunity for all races.

The fact that American ideals are only partly carried out in real life does not **diminish** their importance. Most Americans still believe in them and are strongly affected by them in their everyday lives. It is easier to understand what Americans are thinking and feeling if we can understand what these basic American values are and how they influence almost every facet of life in the United States.

The six basic values presented in this chapter—*individual freedom, self-reliance, equality of opportunity, competition, material wealth* and *hard work*—do not tell the whole story of the American character. Rather, they should be thought of as **themes** which will be developed in our discussions on religion, family life, education, business, and politics. These themes will appear throughout the book as we continue to explore more facets of the American character and how it affects life in the United States.

New Words

censor to examine information and exclude anything that is unacceptable
overthrow to take power away from a government by force; to defeat
profound deep; very important
eliminate to end; to exclude
acquire to get
apt likely
aspect part; facet
peer people of the same age or status
charity an organization that gives money or other help to the poor
hereditary that which can be inherited
prestige honor and respect
abundant plentiful
slogan a popular or well-known saying
tangible real; able to be seen and touched
harsh strong; cruel
diminish to lessen
theme main idea

A. Vocabulary Check

Fill in the crossword puzzle with words from the new word list.

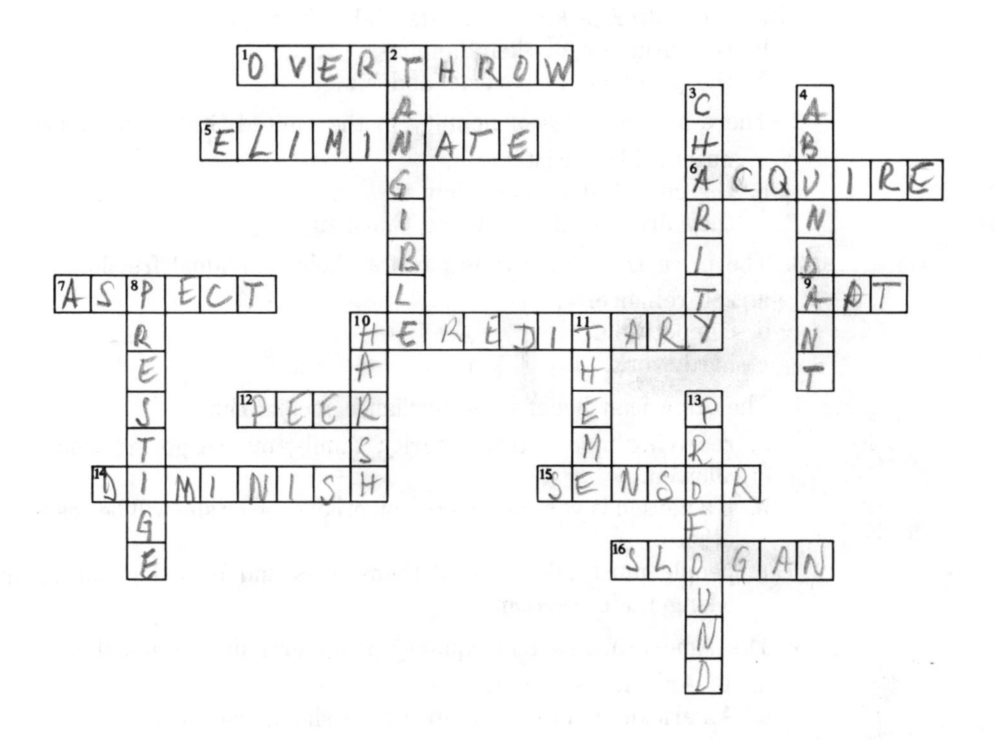

ACROSS

1. to take power away from a government by force
5. to end
6. to get
7. part; facet
9. likely
10. that which can be inherited
12. person of the same age or status
14. to lessen
15. to exclude unacceptable information
16. a popular or well-known saying

DOWN

2. real; that can be seen or touched
3. an organization that gives help to the poor
4. plentiful
8. honor and respect
10. strong; cruel
11. main idea
13. deep; very important

B. Comprehension Check

Write the letter of the best answer according to the information in the chapter.

_a_ 1. The early settlers came to the North American continent and established colonies because they wanted to be free from
   a. the power of kings, priests and noblemen.
   b. the influence of their families.
   c. the problems of poverty and hunger.

_c_ 2. There are no titles of nobility in the United States today because
   a. no one likes aristocrats.
   b. the church does not allow it.
   c. they are forbidden by the Constitution.

_a_ 3. The price that Americans pay for their individual freedom is
   a. self-reliance.
   b. competition.
   c. hard work.

_c_ 4. The American belief in self-reliance means that
   a. receiving money from charity, family, or the government is never allowed.
   b. if a person is very dependent on others, he or she will be respected by others.
   c. people must take care of themselves and be independent, or risk losing their freedom.

_c_ 5. The American belief in equality of opportunity means that
   a. all Americans are rich.
   b. Americans believe that everyone should be equal.
   c. everyone should have an equal chance to succeed.

_a_ 6. In the United States learning to compete successfully is
   a. part of growing up.
   b. not seen as healthy by most people.
   c. not necessary, because Americans believe in equality.

_b_ 7. Traditionally, immigrants have been able to raise their standard of living by coming to the United States because
   a. Americans value money and nothing else.
   b. there were such abundant natural resources here.
   c. the rich have shared their wealth with the poor.

_b_ 8. Americans see their material posessions as
   a. having nothing to do with social status.
   b. the natural reward for their hard work.
   c. no indication of a person's abilities.

a 9. A belief in the value of hard work
   (a.) developed because it was necessary to work hard to convert natural resources into material goods.
   b. developed because the immigrants who came here had a natural love of hard work.
   c. has never been a part of the American value system because people have so much.

c 10. In reality, such American ideals as equality of opportunity and self-reliance
   a. are not real because there is no equality in the United States.
   b. are always put into practice in the United States and truly describe American life.
   (c.) are only partly carried out in real life but are still important because people believe in them.

C. Questions for Discussion and Composition

1. What powers of censorship does the government in your country have? Is there any censorship of radio, TV, newspapers, magazines, books? Do you believe in political censorship? Certain words are forbidden on American TV but not in the movies. Should some aspects of life not be shown on the screen?
2. How much political power does the church have in your country? Is there a state-supported church? Is there religious instruction in the public schools? How much political power and influence does the clergy have (priests, monks, or ministers)?
3. Is there a hereditary aristocracy in your country today? Are there titles of nobility? If there ever was such a formal system of separating social classes, when was it operating? Describe it. Is there any evidence of this old system remaining today?
4. Americans believe strongly in self-reliance and the freedom and independence of the individual. At what age do young people become financially and emotionally independent from their parents in your country? Can most people stand alone and solve their own problems? Should they? Which is more important to you, cooperating with others or having the freedom to do what you want? Is there a price to be paid for self-reliance?
5. Should everyone in a country have an equal chance to succeed, or are there other factors which are more important? How important is the social class into which a person is born in your country? How can a person move into a higher social class? Were most of the people who have wealth and power born into a high social class?
6. Is it healthy for a young person to want to compete? What happens to someone who cannot compete successfully in a competitive society? What

happens in a noncompetitive society? Is your country basically a competitive or a noncompetitive society? What are acceptable ways to compete in your country?

7. What is the "mainstream" of a society? Who is in the mainstream of life in your country? What are these people like? Who is excluded?
8. What is the "American dream"? Do you believe it is ever possible to go from "rags to riches"? Why are material possessions a measure of social status in the United States? How important are they in your country? Can someone be poor and still have high social status?
9. Do you think that material possessions are the natural reward for hard work? Why? Is there any work that should be done for itself without thought of reward?
10. What does "keeping up with the Joneses" mean? What evidence of this philosophy is there in your country? How do people deal with envy in your country? What gives people higher status? What causes others to respect them?

D. Outlining

The American education system organizes information by distinguishing between main ideas and supporting details. That is, there are three or four major points and the rest of the information is given to explain or support these main ideas. It is helpful to students who are studying at American universities to understand this way of processing information, since it is used in textbooks and lectures, and students are expected to use this system in making reports, taking essay examinations, and writing research papers.

It is easier to identify the main ideas and supporting details of a reading selection if we arrange the information into an outline. An outline is like a skeleton—it is the basic structure of a reading selection. The main ideas of the reading can be seen at a glance because of their position in the outline.

In this chapter there are three main sections. Each section explains a belief which brought immigrants to the United States and the price they paid to make this dream a reality in their lives. Together they make up the six basic American values, or beliefs.

The outline below is called a "topic outline." It lists the main ideas in phrases or incomplete sentences. Roman numerals (I, II, III, IV, V, etc.) are used for main ideas, and capital letters (A, B, C, D, E, etc.) are used for the supporting information. Numbers (1, 2, 3, 4, 5, etc.) are used for more detailed information.

BASIC AMERICAN VALUES AND BELIEFS

Introduction: A traditional reason why immigrants have come to America

I. Individual freedom and self-reliance
   A. The early settlers' desire for freedom from controls of European societies
      1. Kings and governments
      2. Priests and churches
      3. Noblemen and hereditary aristocracies
   B. The price for individual freedom: self-reliance
      1. Financial and emotional independence
      2. Risk of losing freedom if not self-reliant
      3. Support allowed but not admired

II. Equality of opportunity and competition
   A. The expectation that everyone has a chance to succeed
      1. Freedom of individuals from excessive controls
      2. Lack of a hereditary aristocracy
      3. Chance to rise to higher social class
   B. The price for equality of opportunity: competition
      1. The chance to be equal, not the right
      2. Life seen as a competitive race for success
      3. The expectation that everyone will compete

III. Material wealth and hard work
   A. The desire for a better life—higher standard of living
      1. Abundant natural resources
      2. The great American dream—from rags to riches
      3. Material wealth as the measure of success and social status
   B. The price for material wealth: hard work
      1. Hard work necessary to develop natural resources
      2. Material possessions as the natural reward of hard work
      3. Material possessions as evidence of personal abilities

Conclusion: The role American values play in daily life as ideals

E. Skimming

Using the outline as a guide, skim the chapter to find the sentence that introduces the following points:

1. The early settlers' desire for freedom from controls of European societies
2. The price for individual freedom: self-reliance
3. The expectation that everyone has a chance to succeed
4. The price for equality of opportunity: competition
5. The desire for a better life, higher standard of living
6. The price for material wealth: hard work

F. Cloze Summary Paragraph

This paragraph summarizes the chapter. Fill in each blank with any word that makes sense.

The earliest settlers came ___*to*___ North America because they ________ to be free from ________ placed on their lives ________ European governments, churches, and ________ societies. They created a ________ nation where the emphasis ________ on the freedom of ________ individual. The price paid ________ individual freedom is self-reliance; ________ are expected to take ________ of themselves and not ________ on others. A second ________ why immigrants have come ________ the United States is ________ equality of opportunity. Americans ________ that everyone should have ________ equal chance to succeed, ________ the price for this ________ is competition for everyone. ________ third reason why immigrants ________ come is to raise ________ standard of living. Material ________ has become the measure ________ success and social status, ________ hard work is the ________. Material possessions are seen ________ the natural reward for ________ work. Although these six ________ values may not always ________ put into practice in ________, they are ideals which ________ every aspect of American ________.

G. Ask Yourself

Do you agree or disagree with each of the statements below? Put a check under the number which indicates how you feel.

+2 = Strongly agree
+1 = Agree
0 = No opinion
−1 = Disagree
−2 = Strongly disagree

	+2	+1	0	−1	−2
1. The welfare of the individual is more important than the welfare of the group.	___	___	___	___	___
2. Our destiny is in our own hands.	___	___	___	___	___
3. People should take care of themselves, solve their own problems, and stand on their own two feet.	___	___	___	___	___
4. Parents should pay for their children's college education if they can; children should not have to work.	___	___	___	___	___
5. All people should be equal.	___	___	___	___	___
6. Everyone should be given an equal chance to succeed.	___	___	___	___	___
7. It is healthy to believe that winning in competition is important.	___	___	___	___	___
8. Money and material possessions are the best indicators of high social status.	___	___	___	___	___
9. People who work hard deserve to have a high standard of living.	___	___	___	___	___
10. If I work hard, I can be a success and get what I want in life.	___	___	___	___	___

H. Ask Americans

Interview at least three Americans of different ages (one under 21, one middle-aged, and one over 60) and ask them about their basic beliefs. Ask each one the following questions and record their answers.

1. Do you agree or disagree with this statement: People should place more emphasis on working hard and doing a good job than on what gives them personal satisfaction and pleasure.

2. Some people say that people get ahead by their own hard work; others say that lucky breaks and help from other people are more important. Which do you think is more important?
3. Do you agree or disagree that it is true in this country that if you work hard, eventually you will get ahead?
4. How important is success? Is it *very important* to be successful in your work, *somewhat important, somewhat unimportant,* or *very unimportant* to be successful in your work?
5. In recent years many of the traditional values toward such things as work, sexual morality, and respect for authority have been questioned by those who think that these values no longer provide good guidelines on how to live and behave. Which one of the following statements comes closest to your point of view?
   ____ Most traditional values still provide good guidelines on how to live and behave.
   ____ Although some traditional values still provide good guidelines on how to live and behave, many of these values are no longer useful.
   ____ Most traditional values no longer provide useful guidelines on how to live and behave.
6. Do you agree or disagree with this statement: Having to follow certain rules of behavior is really to the benefit of everyone.

AS A USEFUL GUIDE TO LIFE

Question: (Hand card) In recent years, many of the traditional values toward such things as work, sexual morality and respect for authority have been questioned by those who think that these values no longer provide good guidelines on how to live and behave. Which one of these statements comes closest to your point of view? . . . Most traditional values still provide good guidelines on how to live and behave, Although some traditional values still provide good guidelines on how to live and behave, many of these values are no longer useful, Most traditional values no longer provide useful guidelines on how to live and behave.

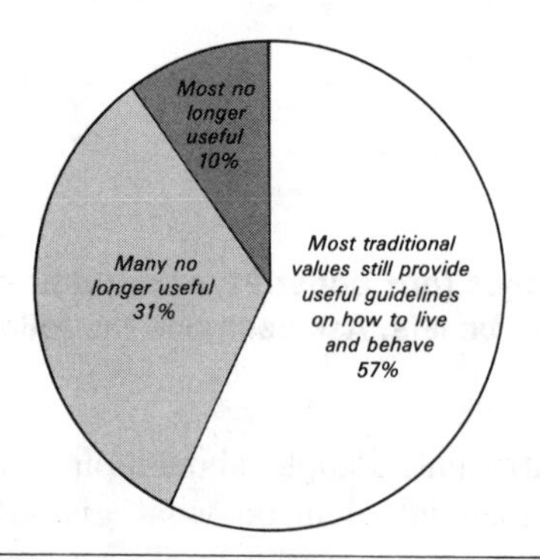

Source: Survey by Yankelovich, Skelly and White conducted for the American Council of Life Insurance, May 19-June 15, 1978.

. . . AND OF BENEFIT TO ALL

Question: (Hand respondent two sets of cards)* Once again, we have a group of cards, each one containing a statement. Would you please read each statement, call off its identification letter, and then the number of the item on the scale card EE that best describes the extent of your agreement or disagreement with the statement. . . . Having to follow certain rules of behavior are really to the benefit of everyone.

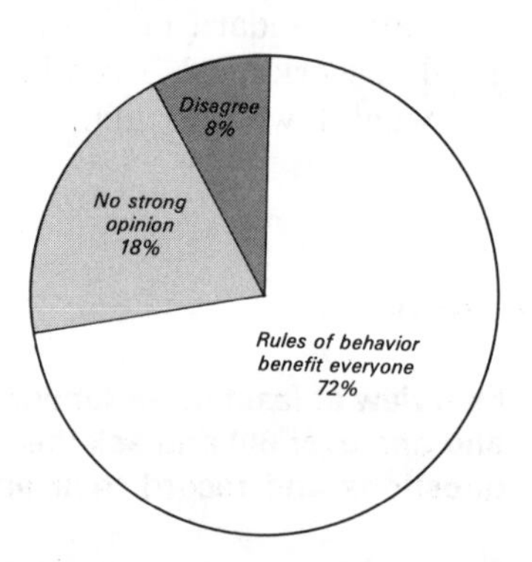

Note: * Respondent given one set of cards with various statements and another card with possible response categories. Agree = Agree strongly and Agree; Disagree = Disagree strongly and Disagree; No strong opinion = Not sure, but probably agree and Not sure, but probably disagree.

Source: Survey by Yankelovich, Skelly and White conducted for the American Council of Life Insurance, May 19-June 15, 1978.

Public Opinion, December/January 1980

I. People Watching

Do this experiment and record the results in your journal.

Rule: Americans usually stand about two and a half feet apart and at a slight angle (not facing each other directly) for ordinary conversation. They may touch when greeting each other by shaking hands (during a formal introduction), or by placing a hand briefly on the other's arm or shoulder (friends only). Some people kiss on the cheek or hug when greeting a friend. Note that the hug usually is not a full-body hug; only the shoulder and upper part of the bodies touch.

Observation: Observe people who are standing and talking. How far apart are they? Do they touch as they speak? What is their relationship? Observe people greeting each other. What do they do? What is their relationship? Observe formal introductions. Do the people shake hands? Do women usually shake hands? If a man and a woman are introduced, who extends a hand first?

Experiment: Ask someone on the street for directions. When you are standing two or three feet apart and the other person seems comfortable with the distance, take a step closer. What is the person's reaction? Try standing more than two to three feet from the other person. What does the other person do? Try facing the person directly as you talk instead of standing at an angle. What happens?

Bill Jackson.

J. Observing the Media

Watch advertisements on TV and look for ads in American magazines and newspapers to find out how American people of high status are pictured. Cut out ads that imply that if you buy this product you will have high status and people will admire and respect you. Bring the ads to class and discuss with classmates the products, how they are pictured, and the messages the ad is sending. The chart shown here may give you some ideas.

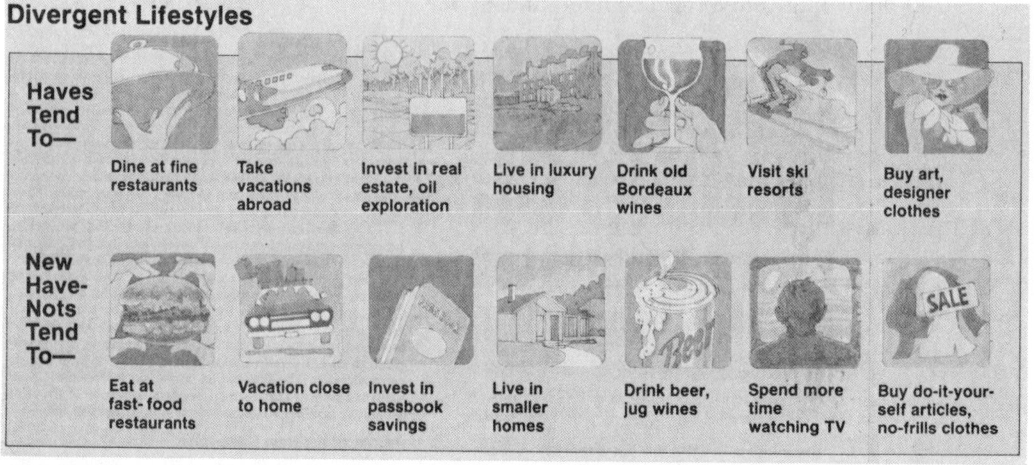

Reprinted from *U.S. News & World Report*, 3/30/81. Copyright 1981, U.S. News & World Report, Inc.

K. Suggestions for Writing

1. Take the responses you obtained from the interviews with Americans and compare them with responses obtained by your classmates. Summarize your findings by making circle or bar graphs which show percents of responses. Study the polls on page 34 and compare the findings of your class with the results of these polls. Are there significant differences? Did you find differences in the responses of older Americans and teenagers? Write a report which summarizes your findings.
2. Refugees from other countries are sometimes puzzled because Americans give them a great deal of help (both financial aid and personal support) when they first arrive but then expect the refugees to be independent and self-supporting after a few months. What American values do you see operating here? Imagine that you are writing a letter to a refugee who has been in the United States for one year. Explain to this person why his American friends now expect him to "stand on his own two feet" and be self-supporting.

L. Suggestions for Further Reading

Mark Twain (Samuel Langhorne Clemens). *Huckleberry Finn.*
William Faulkner. *Absalom, Absalom.*
Ben Franklin. *Autobiography* or *Poor Richard's Almanac.*
John F. Kennedy. *A Nation of Immigrants.*

A Protestant Church in New England. *Vermont Development Department.*

chapter 3

The Protestant Heritage

HOMEWORK

The care of every man's soul belongs to himself.

Thomas Jefferson

During a class discussion comparing Christianity with Islam, a Middle Eastern student raised his hand and asked, "Where is the Christian church in this town?" The teacher explained that there were many Christian churches in the town—Catholic, Methodist, Baptist, Episcopalian, Presbyterian, Lutheran. . . . "Oh, I know about those churches," the student replied, "but where is the *Christian* church?" He expected to find one church with the name "Christian" and was totally confused by all those other church names.

Protestantism in America

To someone not familiar with the Protestant religion, the religious scene in the United States may be confusing. There are two main branches of the Christian faith in America—Roman Catholic and Protestant. The Protestant branch has many different branches or **"denominations."** These denominations have completely separate church organizations and although there are many similarities, there are also significant differences in their religious teachings and beliefs. Some Protestant denominations forbid dancing, playing cards, and drinking alcoholic **beverages**, for example, while others do not.

What causes this religious diversity? Perhaps the major cause is the Protestant belief that the individual, not the organized church, should be the center of religious life. This idea was brought to America and firmly established by European Protestants, and it is one reason why no single church has become the center of religious life in the nation. Instead, the Protestant tradition has encouraged the development of numerous denominations which express the religious preferences of different individuals.

The Protestant branch of the Christian faith broke away from the Roman Catholic church in Europe in the sixteenth century because of important differences in religious beliefs. The Roman Catholic church was the center of religious life in European countries; the Catholic **Pope** and the priests played the role of parent to the people in spiritual matters. They told people what was right and wrong, and they granted them forgiveness for sins against God and the Christian faith.

The Protestants, on the other hand, insisted that all individuals must stand alone before God. If people sinned, they should seek their forgiveness directly from God rather than from a priest speaking in God's name. In place of the power and authority of priests, Protestants substituted what they called the "priesthood of all believers." This meant that every individual was **solely** responsible for his or her own relationship with God.

After the Protestants broke away from the Catholic church, there was much bitterness and many Protestant denominations experienced religious **persecution**. The Catholic church did not recognize the right of the Protestants to have a separate church. Some Protestant denominations were so unpopular that they were persecuted by both Catholics and other Protestants. The result of such persecution was that many Protestants were ready to leave their native countries in order to have freedom to practice their particular religious beliefs. Consequently, among the early settlers who came to America in the 1600s, there were many Protestants seeking religious freedom.

In the previous chapter we noted that this desire for religious freedom was one of the strongest reasons why many colonial settlers came to America. Generally speaking, the lack of any established national religion in America appealed strongly to European Protestants, whether or not they were being persecuted. As a result, although there were some Catholics, the vast majority of the settlers were Protestants and Protestantism became the **dominant** religious influence in the new land.

A large number of Protestant denominations were established in America. At first, some denominations hoped to force their views on others, but the colonies were simply too large for any one denomination to gain control over the others. The idea of separation of church and state became accepted. When the Constitution was written in 1789, the government was forbidden to establish a national church; no Protestant denomination was to be favored over the others. The government and the church had to remain separate. Under these conditions, a great many different Protestant denominations developed and grew, with each denomination having a "live and let live" attitude toward the others. Diversity was accepted and strengthened.

RELIGIOUS PREFERENCE

Question: What is your religious preference—Protestant, Catholic, Jewish, or Eastern Orthodox. If Protestant or other ask: What specific denomination or faith is that? (Hand respondent card)

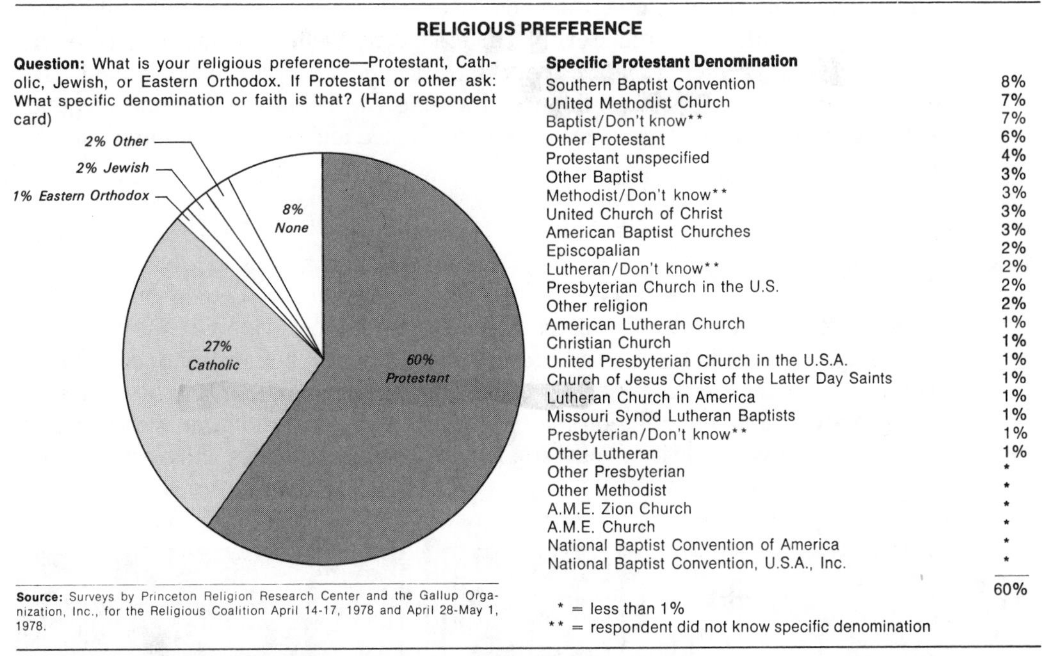

Specific Protestant Denomination	
Southern Baptist Convention	8%
United Methodist Church	7%
Baptist/Don't know**	7%
Other Protestant	6%
Protestant unspecified	4%
Other Baptist	3%
Methodist/Don't know**	3%
United Church of Christ	3%
American Baptist Churches	3%
Episcopalian	2%
Lutheran/Don't know**	2%
Presbyterian Church in the U.S.	2%
Other religion	2%
American Lutheran Church	1%
Christian Church	1%
United Presbyterian Church in the U.S.A.	1%
Church of Jesus Christ of the Latter Day Saints	1%
Lutheran Church in America	1%
Missouri Synod Lutheran Baptists	1%
Presbyterian/Don't know**	1%
Other Lutheran	1%
Other Presbyterian	*
Other Methodist	*
A.M.E. Zion Church	*
A.M.E. Church	*
National Baptist Convention of America	*
National Baptist Convention, U.S.A., Inc.	*
	60%

* = less than 1%
** = respondent did not know specific denomination

Source: Surveys by Princeton Religion Research Center and the Gallup Organization, Inc., for the Religious Coalition April 14-17, 1978 and April 28-May 1, 1978.

Public Opinion, March/May 1979

The Protestant Heritage: Self-Improvement

Although many Protestant denominations exist in the United States today, all of them share a common Protestant heritage. This heritage has been a powerful force in shaping the values and beliefs of Americans. One of the most important values associated with the Protestant heritage of America is the value of self-improvement. Protestant Christianity, like Roman Catholic Christianity, often emphasizes the natural wickedness of human nature. But, as was stated before, Protestantism rejected the idea that acts of wickedness can be forgiven by a priest acting in God's name. Individuals are therefore left alone before God to improve themselves or suffer **eternal** punishment by God for their wickedness. In this way, Protestantism encourages a strong and restless desire for self-improvement.

The need for self-improvement, once established, reaches far beyond self-improvement in the purely moral or religious sense. In the United States the belief in self-improvement can be seen in countless books which explain how people can be happier and more successful in life by improving everything from their vocabulary to their tennis game, or even their whole personality. Books of this type are often referred to as "self-help" books. They are the natural products of a Protestant culture in which people believe that "God helps those who help themselves."

One of the most popular self-help books ever written in the United States was written by a Protestant minister, Norman Vincent Peale. As its title states, it stresses *The Power of Positive Thinking*. The key to self-improvement and success, said Peale, is self-confidence. Reading the Bible is like doing regular daily exercises; it can improve one's self-confidence and ensure personal success in life.

Material Success

The achievement of material success is probably the most widely respected form of self-improvement in the United States. Many scholars believe that the nation's Protestant heritage is largely responsible for bringing this about. The idea of mixing materialism and religion may seem contradictory. Religion is considered to be concerned with spiritual matters, not material possessions. How can the two mix?

Catholics for a Free Choice.

Some of the early European Protestant leaders believed that people who were blessed by God might be recognized in the world by their material success. Other Protestant leaders, particularly in the United States, made an even stronger connection between gaining material wealth and being blessed by God. In 1900, for example, Bishop William Lawrence **proclaimed**, "Godliness is **in league with** riches. . . . Material prosperity is helping to make the national character sweeter, more joyous, more unselfish, more Christlike."

Russell Conwell, a Protestant minister who also preached at the beginning of the twentieth century, gave a speech about the duty to get rich, entitled "**Acres** of Diamonds," more than six thousand times. In it, he said: "I say that you ought to get rich . . . it is your Christian and godly duty to do so." His message was that all men in the United States have the opportunity to rise from poverty to great wealth if they will only use it. He would tell audiences that they had within their reach "acres of diamonds," by which he meant the opportunity to become very wealthy.

Conwell is an extreme example; many Protestant ministers from Conwell's time to the present have strongly criticized the view that God's blessing and great wealth go together. But Conwell's great popularity indicates that he was saying something that Americans liked to hear.

Hard Work and Self-Discipline

American Protestantism, however, has never encouraged the idea of gaining wealth without hard work and self-discipline. Many scholars believe that the emphasis of Protestantism on these two values made an important contribution to the industrial growth of the United States. The Protestant view of hard work and discipline differed from the older tradition of the Catholic Church whereby the most highly valued work was that performed by priests and others whose lives were given completely to the organized church. The work and self-discipline of those whose occupations were outside the church might have been considered admirable, but not "holy."

Protestant leaders brought about a different attitude toward work, first in Europe, and later in the New World. They viewed the work of all men—farmers, merchants, and laborers—as holy. Protestants also believed that the capacity for self-discipline was a holy characteristic blessed by God. Self-discipline was often defined as the willingness to save and invest one's money rather than spend it on immediate pleasures. Protestant tradition, therefore, probably played an important part in creating a good climate for the industrial growth of the United States, which depended on hard work and willingness to save and invest money.

The belief in hard work and self-discipline in pursuit of material gain and other goals is often referred to as "the Protestant ethic."

It is important to understand that the Protestant work ethic has had an effect far beyond influencing only the members of the Protestant Churches. Members of all the many religious groups found in the United States share much of what is called the Protestant ethic. Americans who have no attachment to a particular church, Protestant or Catholic, have still been influenced by the Protestant ethic in their daily lives.

Humanitarianism

The Protestant idea of self-improvement includes more than achieving material gain through hard work and self-discipline. It includes the idea of improving oneself by helping others. Individuals, in other words, make themselves into better persons by contributing some of their time or money to charitable, educational, or religious causes which are designed to help others. This philosophy is sometimes called "**humanitarianism.**"

Andrew Carnegie, a famous American businessman, expressed this idea when he said that wealthy men "have it in their power during their lives to busy themselves in organizing **benefactions** from which the masses of their fellows will **derive** lasting advantage. . . ." Carnegie himself gave away more than 300 million dollars to help support schools and universities and to build public libraries in thousands of communities in the United States. John D. Rockefeller, another famous businessman, in explaining why he gave a large sum from his private

Andrew Carnegie, 1835-1919.
Library of Congress.

fortune to establish a university, said: "The good Lord gave me my money, so how could I withhold it from the University of Chicago?" The motive for humanitarianism is strong: many Americans believe that they must devote part of their time and wealth to religious or humanitarian causes in order to be acceptable in the eyes of God and in the eyes of other Americans.

Born-Again Christians

Perhaps the most dramatic example of the idea of self-improvement in American Protestantism is the experience of being "born again." Some individuals who have had this experience say that before it occurred they were hopelessly lost in their own wickedness. Then they opened their hearts to God and to His Son, Jesus Christ, and their lives were completely changed. The experience is sometimes very emotional. Afterwards, individuals say that their lives are so completely changed that they describe the experience as being "born again."

Millions of Americans describe themselves as born-again Christians, including two recent American presidents, Gerald Ford and Jimmy Carter. Born-again Christians are sometimes criticized for being too emotional and placing too little value on the importance of using one's reasoning powers. It is also said that once they are born again, many people insist on pressuring others to have the same experience, whether they wish to have it or not. Even though it has been criticized, the experience of being born again is an important expression of American Protestantism and its tendency to make people feel a need to change for the better.

A National Religion

In the countries from which the American colonists emigrated, the dominant values of the nation were often supported by an organized national church. American Protestants made certain that no organized national church would exist in their young country.

Americans, however, have developed a number of informal practices which combine national **patriotism** with religion. A number of scholars have referred to these practices as the "national religion" of the United States. The main function of this national religion is to provide support for the dominant values of the nation. Thus, it does in an informal and less organized way what nationally organized churches did for European nations in earlier times.

The informal national religion in the United States mixes patriotism with religious ideas in songs and in ceremonies. The purpose of these songs and ceremonies is to proclaim God's blessing on America and its basic values.

The national religion can be observed on many occasions where Americans gather together in large and small groups—on national holidays, at political

Baseball players stand for the national anthem at Yankee Stadium, New York City. *Ken Karp.*

conventions, at large religious gatherings, and especially at sports events. Before a football game, for example, tens of thousands of Americans will stand to hear a religious leader's prayer, followed by the singing of the national anthem.

Patriotic songs such as "God Bless America," "America the Beautiful," and "My Country 'Tis of Thee" are as well known to most Americans as is their national anthem. These songs are sung frequently on public occasions and may even be sung at Protestant worship services. Such songs express the idea that the United States and its basic values have received God's special blessing.

Some observers of American society believe that the various practices that are called the national religion can have harmful effects. Sometimes these practices can help to create a climate in which disagreement with current national practices is discouraged or not tolerated. In the 1950s, for example, persons who disagreed with current popular beliefs or with government policies were often accused of being "un-American," which meant unpatriotic or even disloyal. Many were investigated by the government, and Americans' freedom of speech was in danger. In the 1960s, young people who protested against the war in Vietnam were considered to be un-American by some. "America—love it or leave it" was an expression of this excessive patriotism.

To the extent that the "national religion" helps to create a climate which encourages excessive conformity with **prevailing** national practices, it can have a harmful effect. However, it usually serves a different function: to express the belief of most Americans that it is important to be a nation of people who believe in God and are loved and protected by God.

The earliest Protestant settlers believed that by coming to America they were carrying out God's plan. This belief gave them confidence that they would succeed. Modern Americans still need to believe that their nation will continue to succeed. The national religion helps to answer this need by reminding them of their religious heritage. It is a means of maintaining their national self-confidence in a rapidly changing world.

New Words

denomination a particular religious body with special beliefs that are different from the beliefs of other groups with the same religious faith

beverage something to drink

Pope the leader of the Roman Catholic Church

solely only; by oneself alone

persecute to treat cruelly; to cause one to suffer for religious beliefs

dominant strongest

eternal everlasting; having no end

proclaim to make known, to declare officially

in league with working together

acre a measure of land (about 4,047 square meters)

humanitarianism trying to improve life for human beings by giving them better living conditions; helping others

benefaction doing good or giving money for a good purpose

derive to get from

patriotism love for and loyalty to one's country

prevailing most common or general

A. Vocabulary Check

Write the letter of the correct definition next to each word. (*Exercise continued on the next page.*)

___ 1. acre	a. lasting forever
___ 2. benefaction	b. the leader of the Roman Catholic Church
___ 3. beverage	c. to treat cruelly
___ 4. dominant	d. only; by oneself alone
___ 5. denomination	e. a measure of land
___ 6. derive	f. strongest

(*continued*)

____ 7. eternal	g. most common or general
____ 8. humanitarianism	h. something to drink
____ 9. in league with	i. love for one's country
____ 10. patriotism	j. to get from
____ 11. persecute	k. helping others
____ 12. Pope	l. to state something officially
____ 13. prevailing	m. a separate religious group within the Christian faith, such as Methodist or Baptist
____ 14. proclaim	n. working together
____ 15. solely	o. giving money for a good cause

B. Comprehension Check

Write T if the statement is true and F if it is false according to the information in the chapter.

____ 1. The Protestant denominations such as Methodist, Baptist, Presbyterian, etc. are all part of the Roman Catholic church.

____ 2. No single church has become the center of religious life in the United States because the emphasis is on the individual, not a particular church.

____ 3. There are no priests in the Protestant churches; individuals are responsible for their own direct relationship with God.

____ 4. Many Catholics settled in colonial America to escape religious persecution by the Protestants in Europe.

____ 5. The Constitution of the United States separates church and state and forbids the government from ever establishing a national church.

____ 6. Protestantism is the dominant religious force in the United States and it has had a strong influence on American values.

____ 7. Protestantism encourages a strong desire for self-improvement.

____ 8. Some American Protestant leaders have said that people who are rich have been blessed by God.

____ 9. The "Protestant ethic" is the belief that people should share their time and their wealth to help others.

____ 10. The national religion of the United States is a mixture of religion and patriotism which expresses the belief that God has blessed America and its values.

C. Questions for Discussion and Composition

1. Which is at the center of religious life in your country: the church or the individual? Explain. Do the majority of the people in your country belong to one particular church or religious faith? Is there a government-supported church?

2. In your faith, if people sin, do they obtain forgiveness from a priest or other religious leader, or must they appeal directly to God? Is there much emphasis on sin and forgiveness of sins in your religion? What are sins in your religion?
3. Is human nature basically wicked or good? What does your religion teach about self-improvement? Are there self-help books in your country? Do you agree with Norman Vincent Peale that the key to self-improvement and success is self-confidence?
4. What is the "Protestant ethic"? How did it help the new American nation grow? Do you have this ethic in your country?
5. What is humanitarianism? Is this philosophy part of your religion? Does it exist outside your religion in your country? What responsibility do the wealthy have, in your opinion?
6. Is there any mixing of religion and patriotism in your country? Are there prayers at nonreligious public events? Where? Soccer games? School?

D. Cloze Summary Paragraph

This paragraph summarizes the chapter. Fill in each blank with any word that makes sense.

Although there are many ___*different*___ Christian churches in the __________ States, the majority of __________ are Protestant denominations. European __________ broke with the Catholic __________ in the 1500s because __________ differences in beliefs. In __________ 1600s most of the __________ settlers who came to __________ were Protestant, and Protestantism __________ the dominant religious influence. __________ there are no priests __________ the Protestant church, individuals __________ alone before God, and __________ is a strong emphasis __________ the need for self-improvement. __________ may improve themselves by __________ material success through hard __________ and self-discipline, by helping __________, and by having a __________ again religious experience. The __________

Constitution forbids government support __________ a national church, but __________ do mix religion and __________ in a form of __________ religion. Its main function __________ to provide support for __________ dominant values and proclaim __________ blessing on America and __________ values.

E. Outlining

Below is an outline of this chapter. The entries for lines A, B, C, D, and E of part II have been left out. Read the outline and go back and find these sections in the chapter. Then look at the list following the outline and decide which entry should be used to fill in each blank.

Introduction: The main branches of the Christian faith in the U.S.

I. Protestantism in America
   A. Religious diversity
      1. Many denominations
      2. Emphasis on the individual, not church, as center of religious life
   B. Origin of Protestantism
      1. Break with Catholics
      2. Differences in beliefs
   C. Establishment in U.S.
      1. Desire of colonial settlers to escape religious persecution in Europe
      2. Colonists mostly Protestant
      3. National church forbidden by Constitution

II. The Protestant heritage: self-improvement
   A. ______________________________
      1. No priest to forgive sins
      2. Individual alone before God
      3. Self-help books
   B. ______________________________
      1. Material possessions a sign of God's blessing
      2. Conwell's urging people to get rich
   C. ______________________________
      1. Work of all men seen as holy
      2. Self-discipline seen as willingness to save and invest money
      3. The Protestant ethic

D. ________________________________
   1. Improving self by helping others
   2. The duty of the rich to help others

E. ________________________________
   1. Ultimate form of self-improvement
   2. Religious experience completely changing a person's life

III. A national religion
   A. Patriotism combined with religion
      1. No government-supported national church
      2. Main function to provide support for dominant values
      3. Songs and ceremonies to proclaim God's blessing on America and its basic values
   B. Harmful effects
      1. Excessive conformity with prevailing national practices
      2. People who disagree called un-American

Conclusion: The role of the national religion

Use the entries below to fill in lines A, B, C, D, and E. The entries are not in the correct order now.

Born-again Christians
Material success
Humanitarianism
Need for self-improvement to be acceptable to God
Hard work and self-discipline

F. Ask Americans

Interview at least three Americans of different ages (one under 21, one middle-aged, and one over 60) and ask them about their religion. Ask each one the following questions and record their answers.

1. How important would you say religion is in your own life—would you say very important, fairly important, or not very important?
2. At the present time do you think religion as a whole is increasing its influence on American life or losing its influence?
3. What is your religious preference—Protestant, Catholic, or Jewish? If Protestant, what denomination is that?
4. Did you yourself happen to attend church or synagogue in the last seven days?

5. How often do you attend religious services?
6. Do you believe in God or a universal spirit? If yes, how would you describe God?
7. Do you believe that there is life after death? What happens to a person's soul after death?
8. Which of these statements comes closest to describing your feelings about the Bible?
   a. The Bible is the actual word of God and is to be taken literally, word for word.
   b. The Bible is the inspired word of God but not everything in it should be taken literally, word for word.
   c. The Bible is an ancient book of fables, legends, history, and moral perceptions recorded by men.
9. Would you say that you have been born again or have had a born-again experience—that is, an identifiable turning point in your life?

G. Suggestions for Research

Many Americans feel it is important to give money to their church and/or to charity. Of all the money that is given to charity in the United States, only a little over 10 percent comes from foundations and corporations. Nearly 90 percent comes from individual contributions.

Go to the library and check *Giving USA*, published by the American Association of Fund-Raising Council to see how much Americans give to charity each year and what their favorite charities are. Look for ads for charities in magazines and newspapers and for fund-raising events on TV and in your community. Write a summary of American giving after you have completed your research.

H. Proverbs and Sayings

Ask Americans to tell you proverbs and sayings about religion, hard work, and saving or spending money. Here are some examples to get you started. Ask Americans to explain these sayings to you.

1. God helps those who help themselves.
2. Early to bed and early to rise makes a man healthy, wealthy, and wise.
3. Save something for a rainy day.
4. Eat, drink, and be merry, for tomorrow you die.
5. Idle hands are the devil's workshop.

Religion At Home and Abroad

The most recent global survey of religious attitudes was conducted in 1975 by Gallup International under the sponsorship of the Charles F. Kettering Foundation. Afterwards, George Gallup issued a report summarizing the findings in this way:

The United States stands at the top of the industrialized societies in the importance religion plays in the lives of its citizens.

The findings from the global study, when compared with earlier surveys, show the level of belief and practice to have remained more or less constant among the American people, while something approaching a collapse of faith may be occurring in certain European and other nations of the world.

For example, the percentage of Americans who express a belief in a Supreme Deity has remained more or less constant over the last quarter century (since 1948), with 94 percent currently expressing such a belief. Over the same period of time, however, belief in God in Scandinavian countries has declined from 81 percent in 1968 to 65 percent. In West Germany, the percentage has declined from 81 percent in 1968 to 72 percent today. In Australia, the figure is down from 95 percent in 1948 to 80 percent in the last survey.

Belief in life after death has also remained fairly constant among Americans since 1948, but in Canada there has been a 34 percentage point drop over this period of time in the proportion who believe. In the Benelux nations a 20 percent point drop has occurred and in the Scandinavian countries a 26 percent point drop.

IMPORTANCE OF RELIGIOUS BELIEFS AT HOME AND ABROAD

Question: How important to you are your religious beliefs—very important, fairly important, not too important, or not at all important?

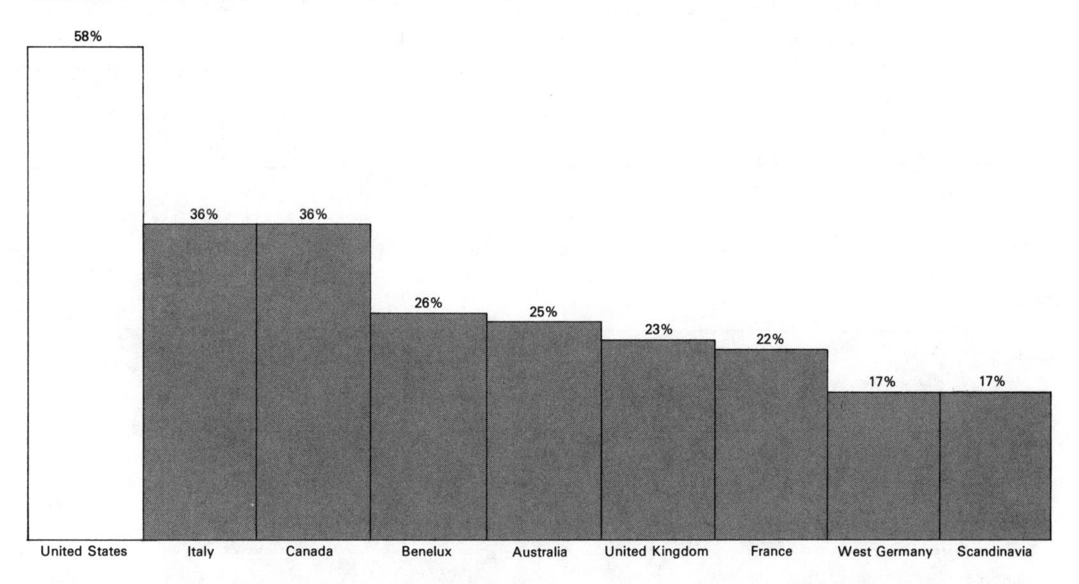

	Very important	Fairly important	Not too important	Not at all important	Don't know
United States	58%	30%	7%	5%	2%
Italy	36	42	16	6	*
Canada	36	36	19	9	*
Benelux	26	30	22	19	3
Australia	25	33	29	13	*
United Kingdom	23	26	26	20	5
France	22	33	23	20	2
West Germany	17	30	37	14	2
Scandinavia	17	28	39	13	3

*Less than one percent.

Note: For India, 86% thought their religious beliefs were very important. For Japan, the figure was 14%.

Source: Surveys by Gallup International Research Institute for Charles F. Kettering Foundation 1974-1975 for foreign; American Institute of Public Opinion (Gallup), January 1978 for U.S.A.

Public Opinion, March/May 1979

I. Ask Yourself

Read the following statements and decide whether you agree or disagree with each. Circle your answer. Divide the classroom in half, one half for "agree" and the other half for "disagree." As the teacher reads each statement, stand on the appropriate side of the room. Compare your answers with the polls.

1.	My religious beliefs are very important to me.	Agree	Disagree
2.	I believe in God, or a universal spirit.	Agree	Disagree
3.	I believe that there is life after death.	Agree	Disagree
4.	It is not important to pray everyday.	Agree	Disagree
5.	It is important to study religious teachings.	Agree	Disagree
6.	I want my children to have religious instruction.	Agree	Disagree
7.	It doesn't matter what you believe, as long as you are a good person.	Agree	Disagree
8.	I could never marry someone of a different religion.	Agree	Disagree
9.	Abortion should be against the law.	Agree	Disagree
10.	Men and women should live together without marrying if they choose.	Agree	Disagree

BELIEF IN GOD

Question: Do you believe in God or a universal spirit?

Believe in god

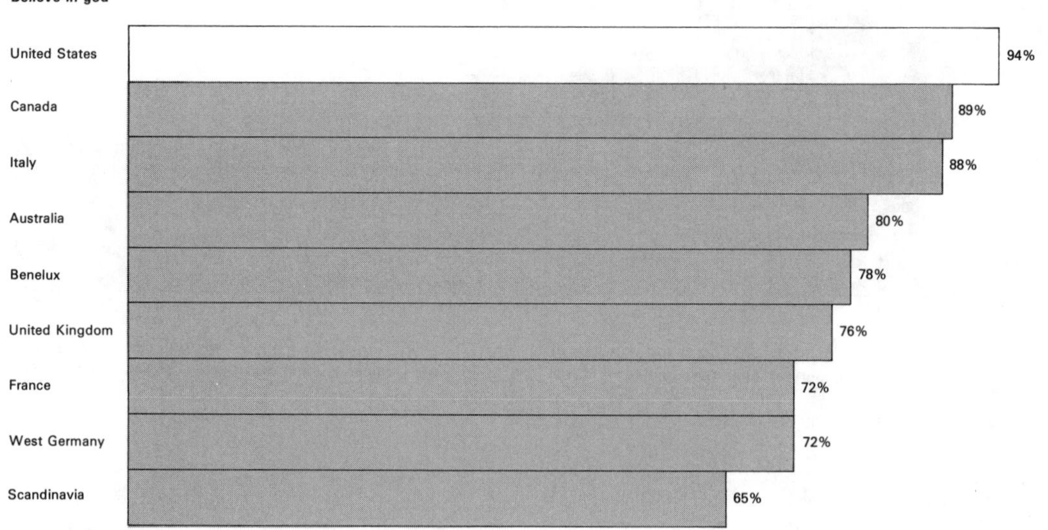

Note: For India, 99% indicated belief in God or universal spirit. For Japan, the figure was 44%.

Source: Surveys by Gallup International Research Institute for Charles F. Kettering Foundation, 1974-1975 for foreign; American Institute of Public Opinion (Gallup), January 1978 for U.S.A.

Public Opinion, March/May 1979

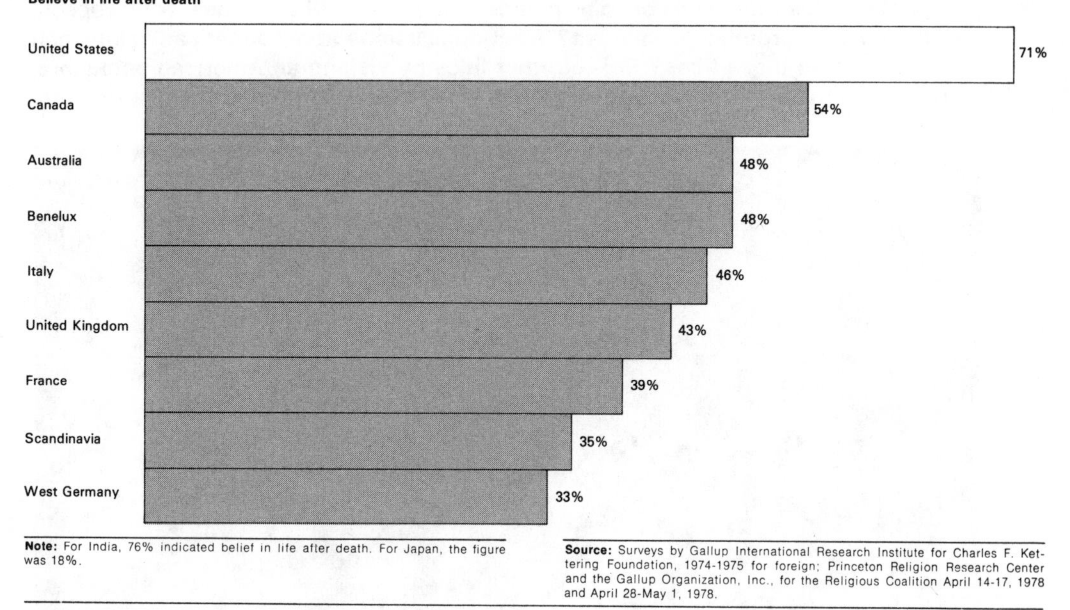

Note: For India, 76% indicated belief in life after death. For Japan, the figure was 18%.

Source: Surveys by Gallup International Research Institute for Charles F. Kettering Foundation, 1974-1975 for foreign; Princeton Religion Research Center and the Gallup Organization, Inc., for the Religious Coalition April 14-17, 1978 and April 28-May 1, 1978.

Public Opinion, March/May 1979

J. Observing the Media

Look at the illustrated titles of some popular American self-help books. What aspects of life do they promise to improve? What conclusions about American values can you draw from these titles? Collect other titles by visiting an American bookstore, checking *Books in Print*, and looking at ads for books in magazines and newspapers.

How to Turn Failure into Success by Harold Sherman © 1958, *How to Succeed at Love* by Michael Zwell © 1978, *How to Start, Finance, and Manage Your Own Small Business* by Joseph R. Mancuso © 1978, *How to Marry a Winner* by Phyllis K. Collier © 1982 by Phyllis K. Collier, *How to Publicize Yourself, Your Family, & Your Organization* by J. Sutherland Gould © 1983, *How to Love Every Minute of Your Life* by Gay Hendricks & Carol Leavenworth © 1978, *You Can If You Think You Can* by Norman Vincent Peale © 1974 by Norman Vincent Peale, *Putting Money to Work* by Yale L. Meltzer © 1976, 1981. Books published by Prentice-Hall, Inc., Englewood Cliffs, NJ 07632. Where not specified, copyright held by Prentice-Hall, Inc. Photo by *Marc Anderson.*

K. Suggestions for Writing

This chapter explains the Protestant ethic, sometimes known as the Protestant work ethic, or the work ethic. Sometimes this belief in hard work for material success or another goal can cause people to become "workoholics" who are unable to stop working, as alcoholics are unable to stop drinking alcohol.

Look for articles on workoholics and write an essay on one of the following topics.

It Is Possible to Work Too Hard
American Values May Cause People to Become Workoholics
How People View Work in My Country
Two Different Views of Work: American and ______________

L. Suggestions for Further Reading

Jonathan Edwards. *Sinners in the Hands of an Angry God.*
Nathaniel Hawthorne. *The Scarlet Letter.*
Nathaniel Hawthorne. *Young Goodman Brown.*
Herman Melville. *Billy Budd.*

The frontier cowboy—a hero of American movies. *Western Film Collectors.*

chapter 4

The Frontier Heritage

This ever retreating frontier of free land is the key to American development.

Frederick Jackson Turner

A Japanese woman was visiting American friends the week the movie "Shogun" was on American TV. While watching the show together, the American woman commented that it was frightening to see the Japanese warriors fighting with swords. "What a terrible way to die," she said. "Do you really think so?" the Japanese woman asked. "To me, it is much more horrible to think of being shot with a gun. Death is so sudden. I think killing with a gun is much more violent than killing with a sword." The American woman was surprised. "I guess it's what you're used to," she replied. "American children grow up watching cowboy movies and playing with toy guns. Guns are part of our tradition. They're part of our frontier heritage."

The Impact of the American Frontier

Although American civilization took over and replaced the frontier almost a century ago, the heritage of the frontier is still very much alive in the United States today. The idea of the frontier still stirs the emotions and imaginations of the American people. Americans continue to be **fascinated** by the frontier because it has been a particularly important force in shaping their national values.

The frontier experience began when the first colonists settled on the east coast of the continent in the 1600s. It ended about 1890 when the last western lands were settled.

The American frontier consisted of the relatively unsettled regions of the United States, usually found in the western part of the country. Here, both land and life were more **rugged** and primitive than in the more settled eastern part. As one frontier area was settled, people began moving farther west into the next unsettled area. By settling one frontier area after another, Americans moved across an entire continent, 2,700 miles wide. How did this movement, which lasted more than two centuries, help to shape American values?

Americans have tended to see the frontier, its life, and its people as the purest examples of their basic values. This has been the **impact** of the frontier on the American mind. For example, the frontier provided many inspiring examples of hard work as forests were turned into towns, and towns into large cities. The race for competitive success was rarely more colorful or adventurous than on the western frontier. The rush for gold in California, for silver in Montana, and for fertile land in all the western territories provided endless stories of high adventure. When it was announced that almost two million acres of good land in

Digging for gold at Gregory, Colorado, 1859. *Denver Public Library Western Collection.*

Oklahoma would be opened for settlement in April 1889, thousands of settlers gathered on the border waiting for the exact time to be announced. When it was, they **literally** raced into the territory in wagons and on horseback to claim the best land they could find for themselves.

Although daily life on the frontier was usually less dramatic than the frontier adventure stories would lead one to believe, even the ordinary daily life of the frontiersman **exemplified** national values in a form which seemed purer to many Americans than the life of those living in the more settled, more cultivated eastern United States.

Individualism, self-reliance, and equality of opportunity have perhaps been the values most closely associated with the frontier heritage of America. Throughout their history, Americans have tended to view the frontiersman as the model of the free individual. This is probably because there was less control over the individual on the frontier than anywhere else in the United States. There were few laws and few established social or political institutions to confine people living on the frontiers. In the United States, where freedom from outside social controls is so highly valued, the frontier has been idealized, and it still serves as a basis for a **nostalgic** view of the purity of the early United States, which was lost when the country became urbanized and more complex.

Self-Reliance and the Rugged Individualist

Closely associated with the frontier ideal of the free individual is the ideal of self-reliance. If the people living on the frontier were free of many of society's rules, they were also denied many of society's comforts and conveniences. They had to be self-reliant. They often constructed their own houses, hunted, tended their own gardens, and made their own clothing and household items.

The self-reliant frontiersman has been idealized by Americans who have made him the model of the classic American hero with "rugged individualism." This hero is a man who has been made physically tough and rugged by the conditions of frontier life. He is skilled with guns and other weapons. He needs no help from others. He usually has no strong ties or obligations to women and children. He is kind and polite to them, but he prefers "to go his own way" and not be tied down by them. Standing alone, he can meet all the dangers which life on the frontier brings. He is strong enough to extend his protection beyond himself to others.

There are two types of this heroic rugged individualist drawn from two different stages of life on the frontier. In the early frontier, which existed before the Civil War of the 1860s, the main struggle was one of man against the wilderness. Daniel Boone is probably the best-known hero of this era. Boone explored the wilderness country of Kentucky in the 1760s and 1770s. On one trip he stayed in the wilderness for two years, successfully matching his strength and skills against the dangers of untamed nature and hostile Indians. In 1778 Boone was captured by Indians, who were so impressed with his physical strength and skills that they made him a member of their tribe. Later he succeeded in making a daring escape. Boone's heroic strength is seen primarily in his ability to master the harsh challenges of the wilderness. Although he had to fight against Indians from time to time, he is admired mainly as a survivor and conqueror of the wilderness, not as a fighter.

The second type of heroic rugged individualist is drawn from the last phase of the western frontier, which lasted from the 1860s until the 1890s. By this time the wilderness was largely conquered. The struggle now was no longer man against nature, but man against man. Cattlemen and cowboys* fought against farmers, outlaws, Indians, and each other for control of the remaining western lands. The traditions of law and order were not yet well established, and physical violence was frequent. The frontier became known as "the Wild West."

Daniel Boone, 1734-1820. *Kentucky Library, Western Kentucky University.*

* Cattlemen were men who raised large herds of cattle as a business and needed large areas of land on which their cattle could graze before being sent to market. Cowboys usually worked for the cattlemen. They would spend most of the day on horseback rounding up the cattle or taking them on long drives to market.

It is not surprising then, that the hero drawn from this period is primarily a fighter. He is admired for his ability to beat other men in **fist** fights, or to win in a gunfight. He is strong enough to defeat two or three ordinary men at one time. He is typically a defender of good against evil, but the principal source of his heroism is his physical **prowess**.

The hero of the Wild West is based on memories of a number of gunfighters and lawmen of the time, men such as Jesse James and Wyatt Earp. Although none of these men achieved the fame of Daniel Boone, the Wild West hero has had more impact on the American idea of heroism than the hero of the earlier wilderness frontier. It is the Wild West hero who has inspired countless western movies and created an American "macho" type.

American "Macho"

Through movies and television programs, this Wild West hero has helped shape the American idea of "macho" or male strength. Until the late 1960s almost all male heroes on radio, television, and in movies had the common ability to demonstrate their strength through physical violence. All were excellent fist fighters, gunfighters, or both. Although some new movie and TV hero types based more on intelligence and moral sensitivity than on physical prowess were introduced in the late 1960s and 1970s, the classic macho hero still dominates American entertainment.

A scene from the 1982 movie SIX PACK.

Through these movies and TV programs American boys are constantly exposed to the fighting rugged individualist as a hero type and are encouraged to develop physical prowess as a part of developing their manhood. Gunfighting is no longer respectable, of course. Fist-fighting ability, when used in self-defense, can be, but in much of contemporary American society its respectability is declining. Now competitive sports, particularly football, are accepted ways for a boy to demonstrate his physical prowess and his manhood. He has to be tough and has to fight to win. The image of the rugged individualist has been criticized for overlooking many factors that played a central part in the development of the frontier. The rugged individualist image overstates the importance of complete self-reliance and understates the importance of cooperation in building a new nation out of the wilderness. Second, because the image is entirely masculine, it overlooks the importance of pioneer women: their strength, their resourcefulness, and their civilizing influence on the untamed frontier.

Finally, the rugged individualist image is criticized because the hero (particularly as shown in movies and TV shows about the Wild West) almost always uses physical violence to settle his problems. Critics point out that this aspect of frontier life and legend has had some unfortunate effects on contemporary American society. On the frontier, every man owned a gun and often used it to solve his disagreements with others. Today more than 40 million Americans still own guns and continue to believe that this is the best way to protect their homes and families from robbers and other dangerous people. Guns are very easy to obtain in the United States. In most of the 50 states a man or woman who has not been found guilty of a crime can buy a gun at a store almost as easily as he or she can buy food, clothing, or any other item.

Many crime prevention experts believe that the widespread ownership of guns in the United States does more to increase crime and violence than it does to ensure the safety of citizens. Nevertheless, the frontier tradition of individual freedom carried to the extreme has blocked attempts by government to place strict controls on the sale of guns to private citizens. Even the Constitution of the United States grants citizens the right to keep and bear arms. The fact that this right is guaranteed in the Constitution indicates the strong influence of the frontier tradition in the formation of the United States. It should be pointed out that most Americans favor stricter government controls on the sale of guns. However, the millions who oppose such controls feel strongly enough about the issue that they have created strong political pressure groups, such as the National Rifle Association, which has worked to prevent any gun control legislation.

Inventiveness and the Can-Do Spirit

While the frontier idealized the rugged individual as the great American hero, it also respected the inventive individual. The need for self-reliance on the frontier encouraged a spirit of inventiveness. Frontier men and women not only had to provide most of their daily essentials of living, but they were constantly facing new problems and situations which demanded new solutions. Under these circumstances, they soon learned to experiment with new inventions and new ways of doing things.

Observers from other countries were very impressed by the frontiersman's ability to invent useful new farm tools. They were equally impressed by the pioneer woman's ability to make clothing, candles, soap, and many other items needed for the daily life of her family. Lord Bryce, a famous English observer of American life, believed that the inventive skills of American pioneers enabled them to succeed at tasks beyond the abilities of most ordinary men and women in other countries. Although Americans in the more settled eastern regions of the United States created many of the most important inventions in the new nation, the western frontier had the effect of spreading the spirit of inventiveness throughout the population and helping it to become a national character trait.

The willingness to experiment and invent led to another American trait, a "can-do" spirit, a sense of optimism that every problem has a solution. Americans like to believe that a difficult problem can be solved immediately—an impossible one may take a little longer. They take pride in meeting challenges and overcoming difficult **obstacles.** This can-do spirit has traditionally given Americans a sense of optimism about themselves and their country. Many would say that if the United States can land a man on the moon, no problem on earth is

A 19th century frontier family. *Library of Congress.*

impossible. In the 1830s Tocqueville said that no other country in the world "more confidently seizes the future" than the United States. When times are hard, political leaders like to remind Americans of their frontier heritage and the tough determination of their pioneer ancestors. The can-do spirit is a real source of pride and inspiration.

Equality of Opportunity

In addition to viewing the frontier as an expression of individual freedom and self-reliance in their purest forms, Americans have also seen the frontier as a pure expression of the ideal of equality of opportunity. On the western frontier there was more of a tendency for people to treat each other as social equals than in the more settled eastern regions of the country. On the frontier, the highest importance was placed on what a person could do in the present, and hardly any notice was taken of who his dead ancestors were. Frontiersmen were fond of saying, "What's above the ground is more important than what's beneath the ground."

Because so little attention was paid to a person's family background, the frontier offered the chance of a new beginning for many Americans who were seeking new opportunities to advance themselves. One English visitor to the United States in the early 1800s observed that if Americans experienced disappointment or failure in business, in politics, or even in love, they moved west to the frontier to make a new beginning. The frontier offered millions of Americans a source of hope for a fresh start in the competitive race for success and for a better life. On the frontier there was a continuing need for new farmers, new skilled laborers, new merchants, new lawyers, and new political leaders.

The differences in wealth between rich and poor on the frontier were generally smaller than those found in the more settled regions of the nation. People lived, dressed, and acted more alike on the frontier than in other parts of the United States. The feeling of equality was shared by hired helpers who refused to be called "servants" or to be treated as such. One European visitor observed: "The **clumsy gait** and bent body of our peasant is hardly ever seen here. . . . Everyone walks **erect** and easy." Wealthy travelers to the frontier were warned not to show off their wealth or to act superior to others if they wished to be treated politely.

The American frontier may not be "the key" to American development, as Frederick Jackson Turner said, but it is certainly one major factor. The frontier provided the space and conditions which helped to strengthen the American ideals of individual freedom, self-reliance, and equality of opportunity. On the frontier, these ideals were enlarged and made workable. Frontier ideas and customs were continuously passed along to the more settled parts of the United States as newer frontier regions took the place of older ones during a westward march of settlers which lasted more than two centuries. In this way, many of the frontier values became national values.

New Words

fascinate to interest greatly
rugged rough; tough
impact the force of an idea, invention, system, etc.
literally exactly
exemplify to be an example of
nostalgia fondness for something in the past
fist the hand with the fingers closed in tightly
prowess unusual ability or skill; great bravery
obstacle something that stands in the way and prevents action, movement, or success
clumsy gait awkward way of walking
erect standing up straight

A. Vocabulary Check

Fill in the blank with the word from the new word list.

1. If someone is preparing to fight, he will close his hand tightly and make a f_____.
2. Someone who shows great bravery or a special skill has p_____
3. A visitor noticed that in America everyone stood up straight and e_____
4. The invention of the telephone has had a great i_____ on life all over the world.
5. Someone who has an awkward way of walking has a c_____ g_____.
6. If I tell you that someone laughed so hard that she l_____ fell off her chair, I mean exactly that—the person really did fall off her chair.
7. The pioneers who lived on the frontier had a hard life, so they had to be tough and r_____
8. If you are reading a book that is so interesting that you can't put it down, you are f_____ by the book.
9. The life of the frontiersman was a good example of American national values in action; the frontiersman e_____ these values.
10. The frontiersman had to overcome many difficulties and o_____ such as clearing the land in order to succeed.
11. Americans like to remember the days on the frontier and they feel a sense of n_____ for the old West.

B. Comprehension Check

Write T if the statement is true and F if it is false according to the information in the chapter.

____ 1. The frontier experience began about 1890 and is still continuing in the American West today.

____ 2. The reason why Americans are still fascinated by the frontier is that this period represents a time when the basic American values were expressed in their purest form.

____ 3. Because life on the frontier was very rugged, people had to be very self-reliant.

____ 4. There are two types of the "rugged individual" hero: the first is a man who fights against the wilderness, and the second is a man who fights against man.

____ 5. The primary qualities of the American "macho" hero are intelligence, sensitivity, and caring for others.

____ 6. It is difficult for the average American to buy a gun, so very few people own them.

____ 7. The right to own a gun is guaranteed in the United States Constitution.

____ 8. The "can-do" spirit came from the willingness of the pioneers to work together on a cooperative project for the good of all.

____ 9. On the frontier, family name and ancestry were more important than what a person could do.

____ 10. On the frontier, there was a great distance between the rich and the poor and social class was more important than in the more settled regions.

C. Questions for Discussion and Composition

1. Which seems more violent to you—seeing someone in a movie killed with a sword or with a gun? Which is more of a tradition in your country? Do children in your country play with toy guns or swords? How do you feel about that?

2. What knowledge of the American frontier do you have in your country? Do you see American TV shows or movies about the West there? Is there anything similar to the frontier experience in the history of your country?

3. Why is there such nostalgia for the frontier days? What evidence of this trend do you see today? Would you have wanted to live during that time? Why?

4. What is "rugged individualism"? Where did the idea come from? What are the two types of American heroes who have these qualities? Where did each come from?

5. What is the American concept of "macho"? How does this compare with your own concept of "macho"? What qualities does a "man's man" have? What experiences help a boy become a man in your country?
6. What qualities do most heroes in American movies and TV shows have? What qualities do heroes in movies and TV shows in your country have? Who are some of your own heroes? Why do you admire these people?
7. Why has the image of the rugged individualist hero been criticized? What was the role of the pioneer woman on the American frontier? How do women in your country respond to the "macho" man? What role do women usually play in society?
8. Do many people in your country own guns? What kinds of gun control laws are there? How does one buy a gun? What kinds of guns are most popular: handguns or rifles? Would you have a gun in your own home? Why? How do you feel about guns?
9. Why did the frontier encourage inventiveness and a can-do spirit? What conditions in your country encourage people to develop these qualities? What other countries do you believe are now known for these qualities? Why?
10. What does this saying mean: "What's above the ground is more important than what's beneath the ground"? Do you agree or disagree? In your country, how much emphasis is placed on what a person can do? Which do you think is more important—who a person is or what that person can do?

D. Cloze Summary Paragraph

This paragraph summarizes the chapter. Fill in each blank with any word that makes sense.

The American frontier has ____*had*____ a strong influence on ____________ values, particularly individualism, self-reliance ____________ equality of opportunity. Individuals ____________ great freedom on the ____________ but they had to ____________ very self-reliant. These qualities ____________ idealized in the concept ____________ "rugged individualism." There are ____________ types of American heroes ____________ are rugged individualists. The ____________ comes out of the ____________ before 1860 when the ____________ was man against nature. ____________ second comes from the ______________ West era, 1860 to ______________, when the struggle was ______________ against man. The Wild ______________ hero is the basis ______________ the American "macho" hero ______________ western movies and TV ______________. He is a fighter ______________ solves his problems by ______________ his fists or his ______________. Guns are still popular ______________ America today and many ______________ own them. The frontier ______________ encouraged inventiveness and a ______________ spirit. There was great ______________ of opportunity on the ______________ and there were few ______________ in wealth or social ______________. People moved west to ______________ frontier to get a ______________ start in life. Although ______________ frontier disappeared a hundred ______________ ago, it still fascinates ______________ influences Americans today.

E. Skimming Exercise

Skim the chapter to find the following information. Indicate the page where each item is found.

1. What happened in 1860
2. What happened in April 1889
3. Who Daniel Boone was
4. The difference between cattlemen and cowboys
5. Three reasons why the American hero image of the rugged individualist has been criticized
6. How many Americans own guns
7. What crime prevention experts think about guns
8. What Lord Bryce observed about frontier life
9. What Tocqueville said
10. What a European visitor observed about the way people on the frontier walked

F. Observing the Media

1. The American cowboy has long been a symbol of the American belief in rugged individualism and the frontier spirit. What is there about cowboys which exemplifies the values discussed in this chapter: individualism, self-reliance, inventiveness, the can-do spirit, and equality of opportunity? Describe cowboys as you have seen them in American movies and on TV shows.
2. Cowboys and the old West are frequently used in advertisements for cigarettes, blue jeans, trucks, cars, and other American products. What image do they have? Why does this image help sell this or that product? Collect examples of ads on TV and in magazines and newspapers that use cowboys or western themes. For each, explain what the message is to the people who may buy this product.
3. Watch American TV shows that have male heroes. How do they compare with the description of American "macho" presented in the chapter? What personality traits do they have? Compare the heroes of several shows. Would you describe them as...

    having sex appeal?
    being admired by beautiful women?
    having no involvement in long-term relationships with a woman (not married; no children; no family)?
    being a loner (few friends, mysterious)?
    having an ideal or a goal in life?
    fighting against injustice?
    being a man's man?
    moving from place to place?
    being good with his fists?
    being good with a gun?

G. Proverbs and Sayings

Ask Americans to explain these proverbs and sayings to you. Then ask them for other examples of sayings about succeeding on your own or being tough.

1. Pull yourself up by the bootstraps.
2. If at first you don't succeed, try, try again.
3. Actions speak louder than words.
4. Life is what you make it.
5. Every problem has a solution.

H. Ask Yourself

Do you agree or disagree with each of the statements below? Put a check under the number that indicates how you feel.

+2 = Strongly agree
+1 = Agree
0 = No opinion
−1 = Disagree
−2 = Strongly disagree

	+2	+1	0	−1	−2
1. I admire the rugged individualist who stands alone and does not need others.	____	____	____	____	____
2. A real man should be able to defend himself well and even win in a fist fight.	____	____	____	____	____
3. Physical strength is more important than intelligence and sensitivity.	____	____	____	____	____
4. It is important for a boy to demonstrate physical prowess to others.	____	____	____	____	____
5. Sometimes using physical violence is the only way to solve a problem.	____	____	____	____	____
6. Carrying a gun is a good way to protect yourself from robbers.	____	____	____	____	____
7. Having a gun in your home is a good way to protect yourself against robbers.	____	____	____	____	____
8. I believe people should not own guns and there should be strict laws controlling the sale of guns.	____	____	____	____	____
9. Every problem has a solution.	____	____	____	____	____
10. What you do is more important than who you are.	____	____	____	____	____

I. Ask Americans

Read the statements from Exercise G to several Americans and ask them if they agree or disagree with each statement.

J. People Watching

Americans are very conscious of space and have a strong sense of territory—that is, the idea that a particular space belongs to them. Children usually have their own room; the kitchen may belong to Mom; Dad may have a special chair in the living room or den, or he may have a workshop. Observe Americans at home, in a public place, or in a social situation to see how they use space. (Watch TV shows, if you are not in the United States.) If someone has been sitting in a particular chair and gets up, does the person tend to come back to the same chair? When someone asks, "Is this seat taken?" what does that person mean?

Conduct the following experiment and record the results in your journal.

Rule: When sitting down at a table where a stranger is sitting alone, an American will choose a seat across from the person or at least one chair away. The space is divided in half between them, and personal belongings must be kept on each person's respective side of an imaginary boundary line.

Observation: Observe people sitting in a public place where there are tables, such as a cafeteria or library. What happens when a stranger sits down at a table where a person is sitting alone? If someone sits down next to a stranger, what happens? How do the people acknowledge each other's presence? Does the person who was sitting there first move his or her belongings?

Experiment: Choose a table where a stranger is sitting alone and sit down in the next chair. What happens? Sit across from someone at a table and put some personal belongings (such as books) on the table in front of you. Push them toward the other person so that they are more than halfway across the table. What is the person's reaction?

K. Outlining

There are two types of outlines: a sentence outline and a topic outline. In a sentence outline each entry must be written as a complete sentence. In a topic outline each entry must be written as a phrase which is an incomplete sentence. The two forms must not be mixed; that is, there must be no incomplete sentences in a sentence outline and there must be no complete sentences in a topic outline. This exercise will compare the two by presenting two outlines of this chapter. They both cover exactly the same information, but the first outline is a sentence outline and the second is a topic outline. Compare the two outlines item by item. Which outline gives more detailed information?

Introduction: The idea of the frontier still stirs the emotions and imaginations of the American people.

I. The frontier has had a great impact on the shaping of American values.
   A. The frontier experience consisted of the settling of the wilderness areas from the 1600s until 1890.
   B. The reason for its great impact was that it represents the purest expression of American values.
   C. Three values are associated with the frontier: individualism, self-reliance, and equality of opportunity.

II. Self-reliance is a strong trait of the rugged individualist.
   A. The rugged individualist is physically strong, is skilled with weapons, and needs no help from others.
   B. There are two types of rugged individualist heroes.
      1. From the early period, before 1860, comes the survivor and conqueror of the wilderness.
      2. From the later period, 1860-1890, comes the fighter—good with his fists and his guns.

III. The American concept of "macho" is drawn from the second type of rugged individualist.
   A. He is a good fighter and a good gunfighter.
   B. This hero image is criticized because it does not reflect the cooperation that occurred or the role of the pioneer woman, and because the hero always uses physical violence to solve his problems.
   C. Guns are still popular in the United States today and they are easy to buy.

IV. Two other characteristics encouraged by frontier life are inventiveness and the "can-do" spirit.
   A. Because there were many new problems and unfamiliar situations on the frontier, the pioneers had to look for new, inventive solutions.
   B. This developed into the "can-do" spirit, an optimistic belief that every problem has a solution.

V. The frontier strengthened equality of opportunity for all.
   A. Because people were more interested in what others could do than in who their ancestors were, there was great social equality on the frontier.
   B. There were not great differences in the amount of wealth people had on the frontier.

Conclusion: Although the frontier disappeared almost one hundred years ago, the frontier heritage continues to influence American life and values.

The following outline is a topic outline. Certain entries have been omitted and are scrambled in the list below. They match entries shown in sentence form in the sentence outline. Using the sentence outline as a guide, decide which topic entry fits in each blank.

Social equality
The survivor and conqueror of the wilderness
Criticisms of the "macho" hero image
Characteristics of the rugged individualist
The reason for its impact
Little difference in the amount of wealth
The popularity of guns today
Three values associated with the frontier
The development of the "can-do" spirit
The fighter

Introduction: The appeal of the frontier

I. The impact of the American frontier
   A. The settling of the frontier
   B. ______________________________
   C. ______________________________

II. Self-reliance and the rugged individualist
   A. ______________________________
   B. The two types of rugged individualist heroes
      1. ______________________________
      2. ______________________________

III. The American concept of "macho"
   A. Good fist fighter and good gunfighter
   B. ______________________________
   C. ______________________________

IV. Inventiveness and the can-do spirit
   A. The development of new inventions to solve new problems
   B. ______________________________

V. Equality of opportunity
   A. ______________________________
   B. ______________________________

Conclusion: The lasting influence of the frontier heritage

L. Suggestions for Writing

1. In an article called "Fly-the-Nest Tests" (*Washington Post,* July 10, 1979) the popular columnist Ellen Goodman deals with a mother's feelings about her daughter's going off to summer camp. She reflects on how Americans teach their children to be self-reliant and self-sufficient. She believes that this philosophy has something to do with Americans' ancestors and how the frontier was settled.

   > The whole country was settled by one generation of leavers after the next—people who moved to a new frontier or a new neighborhood or a new job, who continually left relationships for opportunities. It was considered unreasonable, almost unpatriotic, for parents to "cling." And it still is.

   The result of this is an emphasis on raising children to be independent and separate from their parents. The goal of parenting in America is to make children competent and confident enough to leave "the nest." What do you think of this philosophy? Is this the goal of parenting in your country? Write a composition comparing and contrasting this philosophy of child raising with that of your country.
2. American "rugged individualism" and an optimistic belief in the future is exemplified by the first walk on the moon, the day when the Apollo XI Mission landed, July 20, 1969. What did Neil Armstrong, the astronaut who first set on the moon, declare that day? What did he mean? In what way was it a "giant leap" for mankind? Look at the illustrated ad for a TV special about the moon landing. What values do you see reflected in how Americans feel about the moon landing? Write an essay explaining these values and how the landing on the moon exemplified them.

M. Suggestions for Further Reading

John Steinbeck. *The Grapes of Wrath.*
Jack London. *The Call of the Wild.*
Stephen Crane. *The Red Badge of Courage.*
James Fenimore Cooper. *The Leatherstocking Tales.*
Willa Cather. *The Pioneers.*

The Apollo XI Mission.

It was ten years ago.

Neil Armstrong said, "One small step for man. One giant leap for mankind."

It was one of America's proudest moments. And the culmination of a national effort started by John F. Kennedy.

In the midst of current crises, relive those historic times. When Americans said we can do it – and did. We put men on the moon.

Join NBC News anchorman John Chancellor, NBC correspondent Roy Neal, former astronaut Alan B. Shepard and others who made it all possible.

A one-hour special broadcast marking the anniversary of this historic event.

Join in the nostalgia.

Of the day they landed.

10:00PM TONIGHT

NBC News 4.

PAN AM

chapter 5

The Heritage of Abundance

For millions of people throughout this world, during the past three centuries, America has symbolized plenty, wealth and abundance of goods.

David Potter

An American woman who recently returned from living a year in Europe was discussing with another American some of the differences she had experienced there. "You know one thing which continually amazed me?" she said. "The amount of **trash** and **garbage** we had compared to what the others living in our apartment building had. I would be carrying out several big bags of trash and there would be just one little bag from the other apartment. Their family was the same size as ours, but they had a lot less trash." Her friend asked, "Why do you think that was?" "Well, a lot of what we threw away was empty boxes and cans. I was shopping at the Army PX store and I bought a lot of American convenience food, and it all comes in containers. Our neighbors don't eat much processed food; they fix most of their food **from scratch.** I started realizing how much of our food was coming out of boxes and cans when I saw all that trash piling up."

A History of Abundance

Only a country that has great abundance could afford to throw so much away. America has sometimes been criticized as a "throw-away" country, a land where there is so much abundance that people are sometimes viewed as wasteful.

Scholars like David Potter, an American historian, believe that the abundant material wealth of the United States has been a major factor in the development of the American character.

This abundance is the gift of nature. In what is now the continental United States there are more than three million square miles of land. When the European settlers first arrived, most of this land was rich, fertile farmland. The settlers also found an abundance of trees and animals. Only about one million Indians lived on this land, and they had neither the weapons nor the organization necessary to keep the European settlers out. One writer has said that never again can human beings discover such a large area of rich, unfarmed land, with such a small population and such great undeveloped natural resources.

But it would be a mistake to say that the abundant natural resources of North America were the only reason why the United States became a wealthy nation. The beliefs of the early settlers were equally important.

In aristocratic European nations during that time, the material wealth and comforts of the ruling classes were guaranteed by their birth. Therefore, as Tocqueville said, the wealthy took these things for granted and placed little importance on material things. The poor people in those aristocratic nations also did not concern themselves with wealth, since they knew that they had so little hope of becoming wealthy or changing their status.

In a nation such as the United States, however, wealth and social position are not fixed at birth. The idea of equality of opportunity in America makes the level of material wealth of both the rich and the poor much less certain. At any time the rich may lose their wealth and the poor may increase theirs. Therefore, all classes in American society think about protecting their material possessions and looking for ways to acquire more. Tocqueville believed that this was not so much a matter of greed; rather, it was a matter of their insecurity. People may be naturally insecure when their material wealth, and that of their children, can change so rapidly either upward or downward during a lifetime, or a single generation.

Tocqueville concluded that it was extremely important both to rich Americans and poor Americans to increase their personal wealth and material comforts. Therefore, the entire population joined in the great task of increasing the nation's material abundance as quickly as possible.

Tocqueville visited the United States only 50 years after the nation had won its independence from England. He was impressed with the great progress made in such a short time. Although the country was still in an early stage of development and there was not much money available for investment, the United States had already made great progress in both trading and manufacturing. It had already become the world's second leading sea power and had constructed the longest railroads in the world. Tocqueville worried, however, about the effect of all this material success. In such a society, materialism could be made into a moral value in itself rather than a means to an end.

Tocqueville's concern, to a large extent, became a reality. In the process of creating a land of abundance, Americans began to judge themselves by materialistic standards. Unlike in many countries, where the love of material things was seen as a **vice**, that is, as a mark of weak moral character, in the United States it was seen as a virtue: a positive **incentive** to work hard and a reward for successful efforts.

Americans use materialistic standards not only to judge themselves as individuals, but also to judge themselves as a nation. Whereas many great nations in history have been proud of their military power, the people of the United States have been proud of their nation's ability to produce material wealth and maintain a high standard of living.

From Producers to Consumers

The emphasis on producing wealth and maintaining a high standard of living has not always been the same. Until the 1920s, more emphasis was placed on producing wealth than on consuming it. Before the Civil War of the 1860s, most Americans were farmers. Not only did they produce food, but they produced their own clothing and many of their own household items. For these reasons, farmers thought of themselves more as producers than as consumers of goods.

During the decades between 1860 and 1920, the businessman—the manufacturer, the banker, and the store owner—became more important in the American economy than the farmer. During these years the United States grew into one of the major industrial powers of the world. The people who lived during these years also thought of themselves more as producers than as consumers.

By the 1920s most of the major industries had matured. They no longer caused **spectacular** changes in the nation. There was, however, one major industry which would change the nation during and after the 1920s. This was the mass advertising industry. Advertising began to have an impact on the masses with the invention of the radio. Today, through radio and television, mass advertising can reach millions of people at one time with its messages.

In 1920, radio stations in two large American cities made the first regular mass advertising broadcasts. From 1925 until 1950, radio was a major source of entertainment for millions of American families. Comedy, music shows, adventure stories, sports events, and news reports were brought into homes all over the United States. These programs were accompanied by short "**commercials**" asking the listener to buy a certain product. The entertainment programs were paid for by the companies which were using the commercials to advertise their products.

Television became the major source of family entertainment in the 1950s. It used the same technique that radio had developed: entertainment programs accompanied by short commercials. But television soon passed radio as a source of family entertainment and mass advertising. Today television often draws audiences as large as 50 million people to watch a single entertainment show or sports event. By 1980 about 97 percent of all homes in the United States had at least one television set, and the family TV was in use about six hours a day. Mass advertising reached its peak through television. Today most television stations broadcast hundreds of advertising commercials a day to millions of viewers. The average American sees 50,000 commercials a year.

Ken Karp.

What impact did all this mass advertising have? It created the age of the consumer. Producing goods for a profit was still extremely important, but big producers came to believe that the best way to increase both their production and their profits was to convince millions of Americans, through mass advertising, to consume more products, especially their company's product. Mass advertising helped to shift the emphasis from the production of goods to their consumption. The older picture of the American as producer gave way to a newer picture of the American as a consumer.

Historian David Potter believes that mass advertising in the United States is so important in size and influence that it should be viewed as an institution, such as the school or the church. Like schools and churches, mass advertising seeks to influence the minds and the values of millions of Americans. However, unlike schools and churches, it does not seek to improve the individual. Its only purpose is to convince people to consume more and more products.

The Impact of Television

Critics believe that the control of television by mass advertising has affected the quality of the programs. They are partucularly concerned about the effect on children who watch television, on the average, about five hours per day. Some studies have shown that excessive watching of television by millions of American children has lowered their ability to achieve in school.

Commercial television is also criticized for **corrupting** the values of Americans. The purpose of the entertainment programs, say critics, is nothing more than to get the attention of millions of Americans who will then watch the commercials which go with the programs. To get and to hold this attention, many entertainment programs include a great deal of sex and violence. Critics believe that such programs corrupt the morals of the American people and make them more violent in their behavior. The greatest concern of the critics is the negative effect of television sex and violence on the values and behavior of young people.

Defenders of television say that they are only giving the American public what it wants. Only popular programs stay on television; others are quickly cancelled. Moreover, television offers a wide variety of entertainment, sports, and news programs in the average family's living room at a very low cost. Defenders of television also point out that, for more than a decade, viewers have had an alternative to commercial television called public television. Public television is not paid for by mass advertising and therefore has no commercials. It is paid for by government grants, **donations** by private companies, and contributions from individual viewers who want higher quality television. The programs on public television are often superior in educational and cultural content to the programs on commercial television.

Even though public television is watched by a large number of Americans, commercial television still attracts much larger audiences than public television. This would seem to support the argument of those who claim that commercial television gives the general public what it wants to see.

What American Consumers Like

People in the mass advertising business and other people who study American society have been very interested in the question: What does the American consumer like? Max Lerner, a well-known scholar who has studied American society, has said that American consumers are particularly fond of three things: comfort, cleanliness, and novelty.

Lerner believes that the American love of comfort perhaps goes back to the frontier experience. The pioneers had a rough life on the frontier and very few comforts. This experience may have created a strong desire in the pioneers and their children for goods that would make life more comfortable. Today, the

Americans' love of comfort is seen in the way they furnish their homes, the way they design their cars, and the way they like to travel.

Cleanliness is also highly valued by Americans. There is a strong emphasis on keeping all parts of the body clean. Perhaps the Puritan heritage has played some role in the desire for cleanliness. The Puritans, a strict Protestant church group who were among the first settlers of America, stressed the need to **cleanse** the body of dirt and of all evil tendencies, such as sexual desire. The saying "Cleanliness is next to Godliness" reflects the belief of most Americans that it is important to keep their bodies clean by taking a bath and wearing clean clothes every day. Indeed, many Americans are offended by anyone who does not follow their accepted standards of cleanliness.

Television and radio play commercials for products to clean almost every area of the body. Some time ago advertisers invented the letters "B.O."—for "body odor"—to sell people **deodorants** to eliminate bodily smells. The commercials made B.O. seem like a disease. Deodorants are now used daily by most American

Deodorants and mouthwashes are popular products in the United States. *Bill Jackson.*

adults and are considered necessary. After B.O., "bad breath" is viewed as the second great sin against cleanliness. Countless mouthwash and toothpaste commercials promise to prevent this. Television commercials usually imply that no one can be popular, or even socially accepted, without using the necessary deodorant, mouthwash, or toothpaste.

In addition to cleanliness and comfort, Americans love novelty. They love to have things that are new and different. Perhaps the love of novelty comes from their pride in their inventiveness. Americans have always been interested in inventing new products and improving old ones. They like to see changes in cars, clothing, and products for the home. New models of cars are particularly appealing. Advertisements encourage people to get rid of old cars and try new ones, whether the old ones still work or not. The American economy seems to be based on consumption, not conservation.

In addition to the three qualities that Lerner mentions, there is a fourth quality which American consumers like very much—convenience. During the 1960s, for example, there was a dramatic increase in such "labor-saving" devices as automatic washing machines (found in 41 percent of all homes in 1960, rising to 60 percent of all homes in 1970) and automatic clothes dryers (found in 17 percent of American homes in 1960, rising to 42 percent of all homes in 1970).* In the 1980s automatic clothes washers and dryers are an expected part of most American homes.

These labor-saving devices are designed to reduce the amount of housework that must be done. However, these devices have not weakened the American work ethic. Instead, more than 50 percent of American housewives now hold part-time or full-time jobs outside the home, and the number is rising. For them, devices such as automatic clothes washers and dryers enable them to complete household tasks more quickly and to have more time with the family.

The American desire for convenience also has created "fast-food" restaurants, which are found in almost every city and small town in the United States. These fast-food restaurants, like McDonald's and Kentucky Fried Chicken, serve hungry customers a wide variety of sandwiches, fried chicken, seafood, etc. in five minutes or less.

Like automatic clothes washers and dryers, fast-food restaurants are convenient because they save the American consumer time that would otherwise be spent in such household jobs as cleaning or fixing meals. Convenience foods which are already prepared for cooking, or even precooked, are also available in grocery stores. These conveniences, however, do not cause Americans to be less busy. Rather, they allow them to busy themselves with other forms of work which they find more rewarding.

Thus, the conveniences that Americans desire reflect not so much a **leisurely** lifestyle as a busy lifestyle in which even minutes of time are too valuable to be wasted. Alexis de Tocqueville was one of the first to see in this a curious **paradox**

* Ben J. Wattenberg, *The Real America* (New York: Doubleday, 1974), pp. 89-90.

in the American character. He observed that Americans were so busy working to acquire comforts and conveniences that they were unable to relax and to enjoy leisure time when they had it. Today, as in Tocqueville's time, many Americans have what one medical doctor has called "the hurry sickness."

Fast food restaurants serving hamburgers, seafood, and fried chicken. *Bill Jackson.*

The Ever-Expanding Pie

During the first two hundred years of their nation's existence (1776-1976) Americans were never forced to change their great optimism about wealth and abundance. They viewed it as an ever-expanding pie. In other countries people believe that the rich take a larger piece of the pie and the poor get a smaller piece. Americans, however, have believed that their economic pie would just continue to grow so that all people could get a bigger piece of a bigger pie. This expectation was based on the early experience that as the new nation grew, the pie of wealth and abundance grew at an even faster rate. In the 1800s the nation grew in size as new western lands were settled and became states. In the 1900s, when the continent had been settled, Americans invented new products and techniques of production which continued to make the pie larger and larger. Under these circumstances, Americans came to believe that their heritage of abundance would last as far as they could see into the future.

The belief in an everlasting heritage of abundance had many good effects. It made Americans an optimistic people with confidence that human problems could be solved. It greatly reduced the conflict between the rich and poor which has torn many older nations apart. Perhaps most important, the belief in an always growing abundance gave strong support to such basic national values as freedom, self-reliance, equality of opportunity, competition, and hard work. It seemed to Americans that their high standard of living was a reward for practicing these values.

Falling Expectations

Late in the 1970s, however, an important change in the attitude of Americans began to take place. Most no longer believed that this abundance would continue to expand. During this time it became increasingly clear that the days of cheap and abundant energy, which in one form or another had powered the American economy, were coming to an end. Moreover, the technology of mass production which had produced so much new wealth in recent decades now seemed to bring increasing danger in the form of air and water pollution. Most Americans experienced new shortages through the highest rates of inflation—rising prices for everything they bought—that most of them could remember.

It is not surprising, therefore, that by the end of the 1970s, 62 percent of the American people agreed with the statement: "Americans should get used to the fact that our wealth is limited and most of us are not likely to become better off than we are now." In other words, the majority of Americans had come to the conclusion that the abundance had stopped growing.

Americans had suffered economic hard times before the 1980s, most notably in the Great Depression of the 1930s. But in the past the belief that the United States was, and would continue to be, a land of plenty continued and supported an

A.T.&T. Co. Photo Center.

optimism about the future. During the Great Depression, for example, most Americans believed that with the help of the government, hard times would pass and prosperity would return again.

What is **unprecedented** in the 1980s is the acceptance by most Americans that the United States has finally reached its limit of material wealth and that "our current standard of living may be the highest we can hope for." (Sixty-two percent of the people agreed with this statement in a 1979 poll.)*

The perception by most Americans that their 200-year heritage of abundance may be reaching its end could deeply affect American beliefs and values which have always been supported by the nation's expanding prosperity. Whether these values will remain strong during the rest of the twentieth century or whether they will **undergo** basic changes is impossible to predict with certainty. In the concluding chapter of this book some of the possibilities for the future will be explored.

* *Public Opinion*, December/January 1980, p. 47

New Words

trash; **garbage** waste material to be thrown away

from scratch starting from zero or with nothing; here, using fresh foods instead of processed convenience foods

vice a serious fault of character

incentive an encouragement to greater activity

spectacular grandly out of the ordinary; attracting excited notice

commercial an advertisement on television or radio

corrupt to make morally bad; to cause to change from good to bad

donation a gift

cleanse to make clean or pure

deodorant a man-made chemical substance that destroys or hides unpleasant smells, especially those of the human body

leisurely without hurrying; *leisure* time is time when one is free from employment and duties of any kind

paradox an improbable combination of opposing qualities, ideas, etc.; a seeming contradiction

unprecedented never having happened before

undergo to experience

A. Vocabulary Check

Write the letter of the correct definition next to each word.

____ 1. cleanse	a. a serious fault of character
____ 2. commercial	b. to make something change from good to bad
____ 3. corrupt	c. waste material to be thrown away
____ 4. deodorant	d. without hurrying
____ 5. donation	e. wonderful; attracting great notice
____ 6. from scratch	f. to make clean or pure
____ 7. incentive	g. a gift
____ 8. leisurely	h. to experience
____ 9. trash and garbage	i. something that hides bad smells
____ 10. paradox	j. an encouragement to do something
____ 11. spectacular	k. that never happened before
____ 12. undergo	l. a contradiction
____ 13. unprecedented	m. starting from nothing
____ 14. vice	n. an advertisement on radio or TV

B. Comprehension Check

Write the letter of the best answer according to the information in the chapter.

c 1. The reason why the United States became a wealthy nation is that
   a. the North American continent was rich in undeveloped resources.
   b. the values of the American people inspired them to develop a wilderness continent into a wealthy nation.
   c. there were abundant natural resources and the values of the American people encouraged them to develop the resources.

b 2. Americans who have material wealth
   a. are always respected and admired no matter how they became rich.
   b. are envied but not admired if they inherited the money and didn't have to work hard to earn it.
   c. are not admired if they had to struggle for it.

b 3. Tocqueville believed that in a nation such as the United States, where wealth and social position are not determined by birth,
   a. the rich are not worried about keeping their wealth.
   b. everyone is worried about either acquiring wealth or holding on to it if they have it.
   c. people worry about money so much because they are basically very greedy.

a 4. The people of the United States have traditionally been most proud of
   a. the country's ability to produce wealth and maintain a high standard of living.
   b. the nation's military power.
   c. their great leaders.

b 5. During the period from the 1860s to the 1920s
   a. most Americans were farmers and they thought of themselves as producers.
   b. businessmen became more important and they thought of themselves as producers.
   c. the United States became an industrial power and most people thought of themselves as consumers.

a 6. The advertising industry began to have an impact on the masses
   a. after the invention of the radio.
   b. after the invention of television.
   c. after about 1960.

b 7. If you watch television in the United States today
   a. you will always see commercials for every show.
   b. you can see programs on public TV that have no commercials at all.
   c. you will see commercials on both commercial TV and public TV.

b 8. The advertising industry of the United States
   a. has no control over the content of what goes on TV shows.
   (b.) may encourage TV shows that have sex or violence in order to get the attention of viewers.
   c. does not encourage people to buy new products they may not really need.

c 9. Americans like to buy
   a. labor-saving machines so they can sit around and do nothing.
   b. rare old antiques that are very valuable.
   (c.) products to keep them clean.

b 10. The view that a country's economy is an ever-expanding pie
   a. is held by most nations in the world today.
   (b.) was held by Americans and reinforced by their experiences until recently.
   c. is still held by the majority of the American people today.

C. Questions for Discussion and Composition

1. Which is more important for economic growth: a good supply of natural resources or the values of the people in the society? Give examples. How has the presence or absence of these resources affected various countries' economic growth?
2. Who is more admirable: the person who has become rich through hard work, or the one who has inherited the money? What value is there, if any, in having to struggle in life?
3. Can love of material possessions ever be a positive force? How? How important are material possessions for happiness? What material possessions are truly essential? Should a country make it a policy to try to raise the standard of living for its people?
4. Are there commercials on radio and TV in your country? If so, are they all grouped together at a certain time of day, or do they appear during and between programs? What should the role of mass advertising on radio and TV be? Should the advertising industry be regulated? Why?
5. What is the role of television in a society? What is its role in your country? How is television regulated? What effect does TV have on the morals of the people? Is there much sex and violence shown? How do you feel about this?
6. How do people in your country feel about deodorants? Are they used by most people? Are they advertised on TV? How often does the average person take a bath? What do you think about the American view of cleanliness? In your country what things must be kept clean?

7. Why are fast-food restaurants so popular in the United States? Are they starting to appear in your country? How about convenience foods—canned goods, frozen foods, TV dinners, "instant" foods? Are they popular in your country? Have you tried them?

D. Cloze Summary Paragraph

This paragraph summarizes the chapter. Fill in each blank with any word that makes sense.

The United States became ____*a*____ wealthy nation because of ____the____ abundant undeveloped natural resources ____and____ the values of the ____american____ people which inspired them ____to____ build a land of __________ material wealth. Their belief ____in____ equality of opportunity meant ____that____ everyone had the chance ____to____ succeed, or to fail. ____Then____, everyone became concerned about ____increasing____ and keeping wealth. Americans ____used____ to use materialistic standards ____to____ judge themselves both as ____individuals____ and as a nation. ____To____ the 1920s the emphasis ____placed____ on the production of ____material____ goods, but after the ____begining____ of mass advertising on ____the____ radio, the emphasis shifted ____into____ consumption. The advertising industry ____then____ has control over television ____programs____, and critics say TV ____corrupt____ morals by using sex ____and____ violence to attract the ____interest____ of viewers. (Public TV ____has____ no commercials.) Advertisements appeal ____the____ Americans' love of comfort, clean liness, novelty, and convenience. Americans started to believe that abundance would last forever; now most believe that things will never change any better.

E. People Watching

Observe what Americans throw away. Visit a fast-food restaurant and count the containers that are thrown away from one person's meal.

F. Proverbs and Sayings

Americans have a strong sense of time as a resource—something to be used, saved, spent, shared, etc. How they talk about time is an indication of how they feel about it. Add to the list of time expressions below by asking Americans for suggestions, by listening to conversations, and by watching TV. What value does time have for Americans?

1. A stitch in time saves nine.
2. Time is money.
3. Time and the tide wait for no man.
4. I don't have time for that today.
5. Can you give me a few minutes of your time?
6. We lost a lot of time on that.

1ST COME, 1ST SERVED!

save time

Running Against the Clock

time, money, energy savers

YOUR TIMING IS PERFECT

MAKE TRACKS

G. Outlining

The chapter outline below is a *topic* outline. Notice that all the entries are written as incomplete sentences.

Introduction: The role of abundance and the American values in building a wealthy nation

I. Equality of opportunity and materialism
   A. The effect of equality of opportunity
   B. The growth of materialism

II. From producers to consumers
   A. Americans as producers until 1920 s
   B. The role of mass advertising after 1920

III. The impact of TV
   A. Control of TV by advertising industry
   B. Public TV

IV. What consumers like
   A. Comfort
   B. Cleanliness
   C. Novelty
   D. Convenience

V. From rising expectations to falling expectations
   A. The ever-expanding pie: the belief that abundance would last forever
   B. Falling expectations: the problems of limited resources and pollution

Conclusion: The effect the decline of abundance will have on the future

After you have studied the topic outline above, prepare to rewrite it as a sentence outline. To do this, you must rewrite each entry as a complete sentence. Part of the work has been done for you below. Fill in the blanks by changing the matching entry in the topic outline above into a complete sentence. You may wish to look back in the chapter and skim to get ideas to use in forming your sentence. Remember, the two outlines will be similar when completed; the entries will deal with the same information, item by item. The only difference will be the form in which the information is presented.

Introduction: The abundant natural resources and the values of the American people both played a role in the building of a wealthy nation.

I. Two important values are equality of opportunity and materialism.
   A. The belief in equality of opportunity caused people to want to try to increase their material wealth.
   B. Materialism developed as a value which became an end in itself.

II. In this century, Americans have changed from thinking of themselves primarily as producers to thinking of themselves primarily as consumers.
   A. ______________________________
   B. ______________________________

III. Television has had a great impact on American society.
   A. ______________________________
   B. Public TV is an alternative to commercial television.

IV. What do American consumers like?
   A. They like products that give them comfort.
   B. ______________________________
   C. ______________________________
   D. They like convenience.

V. Americans have gone from a time of rising expectations to a time of falling expectations.
   A. They once viewed the wealth of the nation as an ever-expanding pie which would last forever.
   B. ______________________________

Conclusion: ______________________________

H. Ask Yourself

If you won or inherited an unexpected one million dollars, which of these things, if any, do you think you would do with it? Check as many as you like.

1. Put in a savings account
2. Buy a new home
3. Invest for your old age
4. Start/buy your own business
5. Invest in stocks
6. Take a vacation trip
7. Buy a new car
8. Refurnish your house
9. Quit your job
10. Buy a boat
11. Buy a vacation house
12. Buy a plane
13. Give part to your family
14. Give part to your church
15. Give part to charities

Now arrange all fifteen items in the order of importance to you. Which is the first thing you would spend your money on? Which is the last? Compare your answers with those of your classmates.

I. Ask Americans

Interview at least three Americans of different ages (one 21, one middle-aged, and one over 60) and ask each one the following questions about TV. Record their answers.

1. On an average day, about how much time do you spend watching TV? (Compare your answer with the poll on p. 97.)
2. Do you think you spend too much time or too little time watching television?
3. How would you describe your feelings overall about the television programming now being offered: would you say you are very satisfied, somewhat satisfied, somewhat dissatisfied, or very dissatisfied?
4. As far as sexually oriented material on television is concerned, do you think there is far too much, somewhat too much, about the right amount, somewhat too little, or far too little?
5. There has been a good deal of discussion lately about television shows that show violence—that is, gunplay, fist fights, and the like. Do you think there is a relationship between violence on TV and the rising crime rate in the United States or not?
6. Here are some statements about TV commercials. For each, please tell me whether you agree or disagree.

- Commercials are a fair price to pay for the entertainment you get.
- Commercials are (generally/ordinarily) in poor taste and very annoying.
- I'd rather pay a small amount yearly to have TV without commercials.

LOOKING AT TELEVISION

I LIKE TO WATCH . . . 2 HOURS AND 55 MINUTES A DAY

Question: On an average day, about how much time, if any, do you personally spend watching TV?

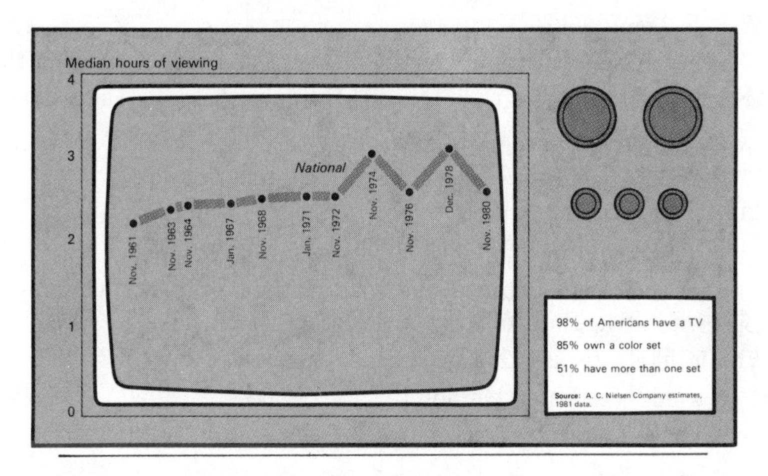

	Nov. 1961	Nov. 1963	Nov. 1964	Jan. 1967	Nov. 1968	Jan. 1971	Nov. 1972	Nov. 1974	Nov. 1976	Dec. 1978	Nov. 1980
National	2:17	2:34	2:38	2:41	2:47	2:50	2:50	3:02	2:53	3:08	2:55
By selected groups:											
College educated	1:48	—	2:04	2:10	2:17	2:19	2:12	2:23	2:24	2:31	2:14
Upper economic levels	2:02	—	2:14	2:21	2:24	2:30	2:29	2:47	2:40	2:52	2:44

Source: Survey by the Roper Organization for the Television Information Office, latest that of November 15-22, 1980.

Public Opinion, October/November 1981

J. Observing the Media

This chapter lists four things that Americans like: comfort, cleanliness, novelty, and convenience. Examine advertising on American TV, on radio, or in magazines and newspapers to see how businesses appeal to these four qualities in advertising their goods and services. Write a brief summary of each commercial appearing on radio or TV and cut ads out of newspapers and magazines. Collect or describe ads for each of the four categories.

Look for these key words and phrases:

1. *Comfort*: luxury, luxurious, elegant, gracious, comfortable, classic, spacious, relax, enjoy, experience
2. *Cleanliness*: clean, deep cleaning, spotless, kills germs, fights odors, germ or odor free

3. *Novelty*: new, different, improved, better than before, brand new or all new, far removed from the real world, exotic, unusual; see, taste, or feel the difference
4. *Convenience*: convenient, fast, saves time, efficient, automatic, ready in a minute or in no time at all, instant, precooked, frozen, heat and serve

Questions to answer when analyzing the advertisement or commercial:

1. What is being sold?
2. What is the main reason given for buying this product or using this service?
3. Are any hidden messages in this ad? How are these messages communicated?

   Does buying this product lead to "success"?
   Will it make you more attractive to the opposite sex?
   Will it lead to "happiness"?
   Will it give you more leisure time?

4. Who are the people in the ad and what do they represent? (Example: A typical housewife struggling to keep her kitchen floor clean.)
5. Who is likely to use this product or service?
6. How would you rate this ad:

   A — excellent
   B — good
   C — fair
   D — poor
   F — terrible

7. After studying this ad, would you buy this product or service? Do you consider this product or service a luxury or a necessity?

K. Suggestions for Research and Reports

Choose one of the topics below as the subject of a report; then go to the library and look for information in magazines, journals, books, and reference texts. Your report should be at least three typewritten pages and should use information from at least three sources.

1. One of the prices paid by a society that becomes industrialized is pollution—air pollution, water pollution, even pollution of the soil. Some of the most dangerous pollution is caused by chemicals and nuclear waste. Choose one type of pollution and report on several magazine or newspaper stories about the problems caused by pollution or what can be done to control pollution.
2. In addition to regular access commercial and public TV, some areas also have cable television. The term "cable" refers to the wire which connects the TV to a system which receives the television signal at a central location. Television sets that are hooked to the cable receive as many as thirty different channels,

compared with the usual five or six available using an antenna. These channels include both commercial and public stations usually available over the air, plus a wide variety of other specialized channels for sports, news, children's programs, religion, movies, and shows. There is a charge for monthly cable service. Look for articles in magazines and newspapers on the increasing availability of cable TV and its impact on television. Obtain TV schedules and compare programs available on commercial stations, public stations, and cable TV channels.

Garbage in a landfill.
A.T.&T. Co. Photo Center.

L. Suggestions for Further Reading

Walt Whitman. *Leaves of Grass* (especially "I Hear America Singing").
Rachel Carson. *The Silent Spring.*
Studs Terkel. *Working.*

The New York Stock Exchange. *Edward C. Topple, New York Stock Exchange.*

chapter 6

The World of American Business

The business of America is business.

President Calvin Coolidge

An immigrant was describing a socialist system of agriculture. "Fresh vegetables are grown on government-owned and operated farms," he explained, "and shipped to the markets for sale. But the production is very poor and the quality of the vegetables is terrible. Do you know where the best vegetables come from?" he asked. "From the tiny plots of land the farmers are allowed for themselves. Farmers are allowed to grow small gardens of their own and they sell their vegetables on the black market." "Why doesn't the government stop them?" his American friend asked. "Because they need the vegetables," he replied. "Even though this privately owned land represents less than 1 percent of the total farmland, 30 percent of the vegetables are grown there."

The Characteristics of Business

Two words are essential to understand the meaning of business to Americans: they are "private" and "profit." Business institutions are directly or indirectly owned by private persons. Private ownership distinguishes them from government-owned and operated institutions. Business institutions also exist primarily to make a financial profit. Their profit motive distinguishes them from nongovernmental private institutions such as churches and charitable organizations which do not exist primarily to make profit.

The Prestige of Business and the Ideal of Competition

The statement by President Coolidge six decades ago, "The business of America is business," still points to an important truth today—that business institutions have more prestige in American society than any other kind of organization, including the government. Americans believe, for example, that businesses are more efficient and well-run than the federal government. Why do business institutions possess this great prestige?

One reason is that Americans view business as being more firmly based on the ideal of competition than other institutions in society. Since competition is seen as the major source of progress and prosperity by most Americans, competitive business institutions are respected. Competition is not only good in itself, it is the means by which other basic American values such as individual freedom, equality of opportunity, and hard work are protected.

Competition protects the freedom of the individual by ensuring that there is no monopoly of power. In contrast to one, all-powerful government, many businesses compete against each other for profits. Theoretically, if one business tries to take unfair advantage of its customers, it will lose to a competing business which treats its customers more fairly. Where many businesses compete for the customers' dollar, they cannot afford to treat them like inferiors or slaves.

A contrast is often made between business, which is competitive, and government, which is a monopoly. Because business is competitive, many Americans believe that it is more supportive of freedom than government, even though government leaders are elected by the people and business leaders are not. Many Americans believe, then, that competition is as important, or even more important, than democracy in preserving freedom. So closely is competitive business associated with freedom in the minds of most Americans that the term "free enterprise" rather than the term "capitalism" is most often used to describe the American business system.

Competition in business is also believed to strengthen the ideal of equality of opportunity. Competition is seen as an open and fair race where success goes to the **swiftest** person regardless of his or her social class background. Competitive success is commonly seen as the American alternative to social rank based on family background. Business is therefore viewed as an expression of the idea of equality of opportunity rather than the aristocratic idea of inherited privilege.

Finally, competition is seen by most Americans as encouraging hard work. If two businessmen are competing against each other, the one who works harder is likely to win. The one who is lazy is likely to lose. Because businessmen must continually compete against each other, they must develop the habit of hard work in order not to fail.

While you're racing after success, retirement's the last thing on your mind.

You're having too much fun to think about quitting.

But someday maybe you'll be ready to kick your feet up and relax on a couple hundred sweet green acres.

You want to be able to take your pick of pastures or castles or tropical isles. And that takes drive.

The nice thing is, you don't have to hide your ambition anymore.

"If you've got it, go get it." That's what society is telling you these days.

If *you're* out there on the fast track, your business reading starts with FORTUNE.

It's the horse's mouth. The authority. The one you rely on when you've just *got* to be right.

It's where you get a vital couple of steps on the competition. In management, technology, the economy, *everything*.

FORTUNE's how to make it. And keep it.

And it's where to put your advertising if you want to succeed with the fast-track people.

FORTUNE
How to succeed.

Americans are aware that business institutions often do not live up to the ideals of competition and the support of freedom, equality of opportunity, and hard work. There is a side of Americans that distrusts the motives of businessmen. Even with these **flaws**, however, most Americans believe that business comes closer than other institutions to carrying out competition and other basic values in daily practice.

Are capitalists greedy businessmen only interested in money, or are they the providers of great gifts to make life better for all? *Public Opinion, April/May 1981.*

The Prestige of Business and the Dream of Getting Rich

There is a second reason for the respect business institutions receive in the United States. The American dream has always been to rise from poverty or modest wealth to great wealth. In the United States this has usually been accomplished through successful business careers. All of the great private fortunes in the nation were built by successful businessmen, many of whom started life with very little. Careers in business still offer the greatest opportunity for the ambitious individual to become wealthy.

Alexis de Tocqueville observed the great attractiveness of business careers for Americans as early as the 1830s. Americans strongly preferred business to farming, he said, because business offered the opportunity to get rich more quickly. Even those who were farmers were possessed with a strong business spirit. They often ran small businesses to add to the money they made from farming. Tocqueville also noticed that American farmers were often more interested in buying and selling land for a profit than in farming it. Thus, even in Tocqueville's day when most Americans were still farmers, the seeds of a business civilization had already been planted.

Not only is business seen as the best way for individuals to become rich, it provides the best way for making the entire nation rich. Through competition, more people become richer. By contrast, a socialistic system of production and distribution of goods (one that is owned and operated by the government) is seen as greatly inferior. A socialistic system is distrusted because of the monopoly of power held by the government which eliminates competition. There are few countries, if any, in the world where business institutions are so strongly preferred over government institutions as agencies for producing and distributing goods. In a recent poll Americans were asked, "Would you favor or oppose introducing socialism in the United States?" Only 10 percent replied that they would favor socialism, while 62 percent said they were opposed to it.*

Two Kinds of American Business Heroes

Because of the many beliefs that connect business to the wealth and the basic values of the United States, the successful businessman has become a kind of hero to the American people. Two kinds of businessman-heroes have gained widespread respect among the people. The first kind is often called "the **entrepreneur**." Because he is viewed as an example of basic American values in their pure form, he will be described here as the pure hero. The second kind of hero is often called "the organization man." He is seen as a less perfect example of basic American values but still commands great respect.

The Entrepreneur as Hero

The entrepreneur is the purest kind of businessman-hero for a number of reasons. The first reason is that he succeeds in building something great out of nothing. The men who more than one hundred years ago built up the great

* *Public Opinion*, July/August 1978, pp. 41-42.

industries of the nation, such as steel, railroads, and oil refining, were usually entrepreneurs. They started with very little money or power and ended as the heads of huge companies which earned enormous fortunes.

The fact that these early entrepreneurs built great industries out of very little made them seem to millions of Americans like the heroes of the early frontier days who went into the vast wilderness of the United States and turned forests into farms, villages, and small cities. The entrepreneur, like the earlier hero of the frontier, was seen as a "rugged individual."

Because the entrepreneur made so much out of so little, he became a hero to the common man in America. The entrepreneur often began as a common man himself; without the aid of inherited social title or inherited money, he became a "self-made" millionaire. He was thus a perfect example of the American ideal of equality of opportunity in action.

The strong influence of the success stories of the early entrepreneurs on the masses of Americans can be found in the great popularity of the novels of Horatio Alger, which were published in late nineteenth- and early twentieth-century America. About 17 million copies of these books were sold to the American public. The central theme of Alger's novels is that in the United States a poor city boy or a poor farm boy can become a wealthy and successful businessman if he works hard and relies on himself rather than depending on others. This is because the United States is a land of equality of opportunity where everyone has a chance to succeed.

In Alger's first published novel, "Ragged Dick," a poor city boy who shines shoes for a living becomes Richard Hunter, a successful and wealthy businessman. The hero rises "from rags to riches" and fulfills the American dream. Dick succeeds only partly because he lives in a land of equality of opportunity. His success is also due to the fact that he practices the American virtues of self-reliance and hard work. According to Alger, Dick "knew that he had only himself to depend upon, and he determined to make the most of himself . . . which is the secret of success in nine cases out of ten." Dick was also a hard-working shoe shine boy, "energetic and on the **alert** for business." This quality marked him for success, explained Alger, because "in the **boot-blacking** business, as well as in the higher **vocations**, the same rule prevails, that energy and industry are rewarded, and **indolence** suffers."

Although Americans today are likely to think that Horatio Alger's stories are too good to be true, they continue to be inspired by the idea of earning wealth and success as an entrepreneur who "makes it on his own." A final characteristic of the entrepreneur which appeals to most Americans is his strong dislike of **submitting** to higher authority (particularly the government) and his strong need to escape from it. Throughout their history, the American people have had this trait. They have strongly admired the entrepreneur who conducts his business and his life without taking orders from anyone above him. Americans have great respect for those who can say, "I am my own boss."

The Organization Man as Hero

The great entrepreneurs of the late nineteenth century built huge business organizations which needed a new generation of business leaders to run them. These leaders have often been called "organization men." They also are heroes to

Americans in the sense that they are models of the height of success in American society.

They acquire power and wealth, but they do not have as strong a hero image as does the entrepreneur, because they are not seen as pure examples of American ideals. Unlike the entrepreneur, the organization man does not build a great organization out of nothing. He takes over and directs a great organization that was built by another man, the original entrepreneur.

Moreover, the organization men of the twentieth century do not provide such inspiring examples of equality of opportunity or freedom from higher authority as did the entrepreneurs of the late nineteenth century. Generally speaking, fewer organization men than entrepreneurs have risen to success from backgrounds of poverty. Moreover, the organization man is not his own boss. He rises to the top of his business organization, not simply on the basis of his own abilities, but on the basis of his ability to please those above him in the organization. Once at the top, he is still not his own boss. Typically he shares leadership with other organization men who make decisions as a group. The entrepreneur, on the other hand, was the sole and undisputed captain of his business.

Therefore, the organization man does not inspire Americans as does the successful entrepreneur. In America today, however, the most promising road to success is that of rising through a large business organization. It is extremely difficult today for an entrepreneur to build a great organization out of almost nothing. He is lucky if he can avoid complete failure and instead build a moderately successful business. However, the entrepreneur is still an inspiring model to Americans.

The Decline of the Businessman as Hero

During the twentieth century the heroic image of the American businessman has declined. The change in business leaders from the inspiring entrepreneurs to the less inspiring organization men is only part of the reason for this. The prestige of the American businessman was greatly damaged by the Great Depression of the 1930s. During that decade the nation suffered the worst economic conditions of its entire history. Businessmen had been given most of the credit for the nation's prosperity before the 1930s, and during the Great Depression they received most of the blame for the hard times.

The prestige of businessmen and their heroic image suffered greatly as a result. Joseph Kennedy, Sr., a very wealthy and successful entrepreneur (and the father of President John F. Kennedy), had a clear understanding of what happened to the successful businessman. "... his moral prestige is gone," wrote Kennedy. "He is made to doubt ... that he represents the American system in its most perfect expression."

The Great Depression was a terrible blow for business leaders. Before the 1930s they had been the dominant power in the United States. During and after the 1930s they had to share that power with a rapidly expanding national government. Nevertheless, business has continued to be a powerful force in the United States. Even though the American people are increasingly critical of business, they retain the view that business, largely because of its competitive nature, is the most efficient way to produce material goods and services. They strongly prefer that business do these things rather than the national government. Ralph Nader, who is known in the United States as a strong critic of business, put it this way: "The only thing worse than having a car built by General Motors is to have one built by the government."

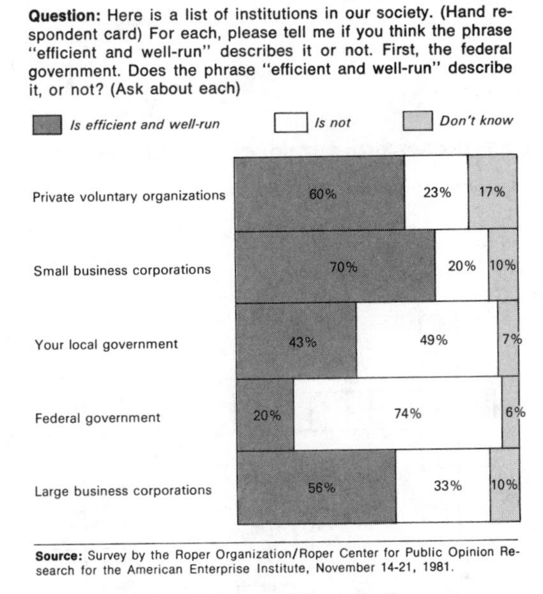

Public Opinion, February/March 1982

It is also true that while Americans are often distrustful of the motives of businessmen as individuals, they continue to believe in an economic system based mainly on private business organizations which operate for a profit. Polls taken in the late 1970s, for example, found that over 90 percent of the American public agreed with the statement, "We must be ready to make sacrifices if necessary to preserve the free enterprise system."* The statement made by President Calvin Coolidge six decades ago, that "the business of America is business" is still largely true today.

* *Public Opinion*, July/August 1978, p. 42.

New Words

swiftest fastest
flaw imperfection; a small sign of damage that makes an object not perfect
entrepreneur a person who makes the plans for a business and gets it going
on the alert quick to see and act
boot-blacking shoe shining
vocation occupation; a person's work or employment
indolence laziness
submit to agree to obey

A. Vocabulary Check

Fill in the crossword puzzle with words from the new word list.

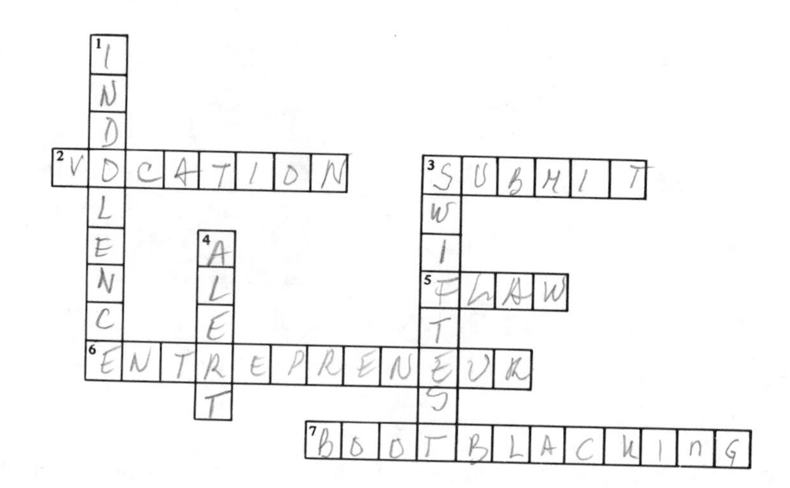

ACROSS

2. occupation
3. to agree to obey
5. an imperfection
6. someone who starts a new business
7. shining shoes

DOWN

1. laziness
3. fastest
4. quick to see and act

B. Comprehension Check

Write T if the statement is true and F if it is false according to the information in the chapter.

____ 1. Most American businesses are directly or indirectly owned by the government.

____ 2. Business has great prestige because Americans believe that it supports ideals and values which are important to the country.

____ 3. Americans believe that competition among businesses is good for the economy but it does little to protect the freedom of the individual.

____ 4. To succeed in American business, people believe that family background and social position are more important than anything, including hard work.

____ 5. Most Americans believe that success in business offers the best chance to fulfill the dream of being wealthy.

____ 6. The business spirit is relatively new in America: it began after World War II.

____ 7. The "organization man" is the most admired businessman-hero since he is the one who has started a successful business from practically nothing.

____ 8. Horatio Alger's books were so popular because they told stories of men who went from rags to riches by starting successful businesses from practically nothing.

____ 9. Most successful businesses today are run by "organization men" and not entrepreneurs.

____ 10. Although Americans may not be convinced that the free enterprise system is the best for the economy, they do have an ever-increasing respect and admiration for the moral leadership of businessmen in their society.

C. Questions for Discussion and Composition

1. Do you think people are motivated to work harder when they will increase personal profit, or when they are working together toward a common goal under a socialist system? Is the economy of your country basically capitalist or socialist? What are the advantages and disadvantages of both?

2. What kind of respect do businesses and businesspeople have in your country? Why is this so? Do businesses compete with each other? Do you think competition among businesses benefits the customer? Why?

3. Why do Americans believe that competition among businesses protects the freedom of the individual? Are there any large monopolies in your country? Are monopolies good or bad for the customer? Why?
4. Why do Americans believe that competition among businesses strengthens the ideal of equality of opportunity? If you were looking for a job with a business in your country, how would you go about it? How important are family reputation and connections?
5. What is the best way to get rich in your country? Is it through a business career? What kinds of business career opportunities are there in your country? Which ones promise the most money?
6. Which is a better agency for producing and distributing goods—business or the government? Why? Are there aspects of producing or distributing goods that can be better done by one or the other? Should both have a role?
7. What is the difference between an entrepreneur and an organization man? Which person do you admire more? Who would you rather be? Which person takes greater risks? Why do Americans look at the successful entrepreneur as a hero?
8. Who was Horatio Alger? Why do you think his stories were so popular? Would they be popular in your country? Why? What values do the stories emphasize?
9. Why has respect for the businessperson declined in America? Do you agree with Ralph Nader? Would you buy a car built by the government of your country?
10. What qualities should a good businessperson have, in your opinion? Would you want to work for a person like that? What personal qualities would you like your boss to have? How would you feel about having a woman as your boss?

D. Cloze Summary Paragraph

This paragraph summarizes the chapter. Fill in each blank with any word that makes sense.

American businesses are privately ___*owned*___ and are operated for ________ profit. Americans have high ________ for business because they ________ business competition protects the ________ American values of individual ________, equality of opportunity, and ________ work. Business is also ________ because Americans believe it ________ the best opportunity for ________ individuals and the nation ________ a whole to become ________. For these reasons, businessmen ________ become heroes. Entrepreneurs are ________ most respected heroes because ________ build a successful business ________ nothing. They are self-made ________ who are their own ________. Horatio Alger wrote many ________ stories about such men ________ went from rags to ________. Nowadays business heroes are ________ likely to be organization ________ who take over and ________ large organizations started by ________. Few rise from poverty, ________ they must cooperate with ________ organization leaders. After the ________ Depression of the 1930s ________ lost respect and power. ________ were blamed for economic ________ times and they had ________ share their power with ________ newly expanding national government. ________ even though Americans sometimes ________ businessmen, they still believe ________ in the free enterprise ________ as best for the ________.

E. Outlining

The following outline of the chapter is a topic outline. The main ideas are all there, but some of the supporting details have been omitted. Skim the chapter to find the missing information and fill in the blanks to complete the outline. Be sure that each entry is a phrase and *not* a complete sentence.

Introduction: The characteristics of American business

I. The prestige of business and the ideal of competition
  A. Why business has high prestige
    1. ______________________________
    2. ______________________________
  B. The role of competition in protecting American values
    1. Individual freedom
    2. ______________________________
    3. ______________________________

II. The prestige of business and the dream of getting rich
  A. The opportunity business offers for individuals
    1. ______________________________
    2. ______________________________
  B. Tocqueville's observation of the business spirit
    1. Business preferred over farming for getting rich
    2. Small businesses run by many farmers
  C. The opportunity business offers to the nation as a whole
    1. ______________________________
    2. ______________________________

III. Two kinds of American business heroes
  A. The entrepreneur
    1. Builds something out of nothing
    2. A self-made man
      a. Rises from poverty
      b. Hero of Horatio Alger stories
    3. Dislikes submitting to higher authority
  B. The organization man
    1. ______________________________
    2. ______________________________
    3. ______________________________
    4. More common today than entrepreneur

IV. The decline of the businessman as hero
  A. The effect of the Great Depression
    1. ______________________________
    2. ______________________________
  B. The loss of power of business
    1. ______________________________
    2. ______________________________

Conclusion: Private enterprise still seen as best system for U.S. today

F. Ask Yourself

Do you agree or disagree with each of the statements below? Put a check under the number that indicates how you feel:

+2 = Strongly agree
+1 = Agree
0 = No opinion or don't know
−1 = Disagree
−2 = Strongly disagree

	+2	+1	0	−1	−2
1. Businesspeople who start a successful business from scratch are heroes.	___	___	___	___	___
2. I admire a person who is his or her boss more than an organization man who must answer to others.	___	___	___	___	___
3. I would like to own my own business.	___	___	___	___	___
4. A medical doctor has more prestige than a businessperson.	___	___	___	___	___
5. Women and men make equally good bosses.	___	___	___	___	___
6. I would rather have a man for a boss than a woman.	___	___	___	___	___
7. The place where I live is more important to me personally than where I work.	___	___	___	___	___
8. I would take a job I liked for less pay over a job I didn't like for more pay.	___	___	___	___	___
9. I would work on an assembly line in a factory if the pay were good.	___	___	___	___	___
10. All things considered, socialism is better for a country and its people than capitalism.	___	___	___	___	___

G. People Watching

Who works in the United States? What ages? Men, women, teenagers, the elderly? What kind of jobs do they do? To answer these questions, if you are in the United States, look around you in various businesses open to the public: restaurants, banks, stores, drug stores, supermarkets, clubs, dry cleaners, doctors' offices, theaters, etc. If you are near a university, check to see who is working in the library and the cafeteria. (If you are not in the United States, you may get information from Americans in your country or by watching American TV commercials, reading newspapers or magazines, and doing research in the library.)

Observe people working in at least ten different places and record your results in this chart:

	Kind of Job	Sex of Workers	Age of Workers	Other Things of Note
1.	Teacher	FEMALE	32	work with smile
2.	Teacher	MALE	30	Make his work funny.
3.	Cashier	FEMALE	23	look stressed.
4.	Pizza sales	FEMALE	19	look busy to look to her clients.
5.	Book classifier	FEMALE	21	Look very young.
6.	Computer-information	FEMALE	22	→ possess her job ⇒ teach me instead of help I asked for.
7.				
8.				
9.				
10.				

H. Ask Americans

Interview at least three Americans of different ages (one under 21, one middle-aged, and one over 60) and ask them about their work. Ask each one the following questions and record their answers.

1. What is your present employment? How long have you worked there? Is this a job you plan to keep indefinitely?
2. What other jobs have you had? Did you work to earn money as a child, teenager, or college student?
3. Would you consider the job you now have to be a permanent job? Do you expect to continue doing the kind of work you're doing now indefinitely?
4. Do you have a college degree or vocational training for the job you hold now? How useful is a college degree in your line of work?
5. Have you ever changed careers? Would you ever consider doing so?
6. Is it good to change jobs?

7. When should people change jobs—under what circumstances and for what reasons?
8. Can a person change jobs too often?

I. Suggestions for Writing

Choose one of the following topics and write a composition.

1. Compare the way American businesses operate with the way businesses operate in your country. For example, compare a typical transaction at a shop. How do the activities differ? Consider these points:
   a. When the employees work
   b. Who the employees are
   c. The pace of the business transaction
   d. Whether the shopkeeper waits on one person at a time or several
   e. The atmosphere of the shop
   f. Whether the employees know the customers or not
   g. How long the employees have worked there
   h. The relationship between the employees and their employer
2. Americans believe in "upward mobility," that is, in moving up the ladder of success within a business or changing jobs in order to move up. What American values do you see in this philosophy: self-reliance, optimism, a belief in progress, competition? Discuss the concept of upward mobility and compare it with the system in your country.
3. How do you believe upward mobility affects the way employers treat their employees? Do you think there would be a difference in the attitudes employers have about employees if they knew that these employees would work for them all their lives? Compare and contrast these two systems: a system where employees are guaranteed lifetime employment versus one in which employees change jobs in order to advance to a higher position.
4. Camus said, "Without work all life goes rotten. But when work is soulless, life stifles and dies." What kind of work is "soulless"? When does work "stifle" and kill?

J. What's Your Opinion?

Most businesses in America require those applying for a job to submit a resumé, that is, a summary of their work experience, education and qualifications. Jerrold G. Simon, Ed. D., psychologist and career development specialist at Harvard

Business School, who has counseled over a thousand people in their search for jobs, has written an article to tell you how to go after the job you really want. The article, "How to Write a Resumé," was printed as an advertisement in a news magazine.* Throughout the article is the implied message, "You must sell yourself." That is, you must assert yourself and convince a prospective employer that you are the best person for the job:

> 'Who am I? What do I want to do?' Writing your resumé forces you to think about yourself.
>
> The most qualified people don't always get the job. It goes to the person who presents himself most persuasively in person and on paper. So don't just list where you were and what you did. This is your chance to tell *how well you did.* Were you the best salesman? Did you cut operating costs? Give numbers, statistics, percentages, increases in sales or profits.

Would following this advice get you a good job in your country? What American values do you see at work here? If you were trying to "sell yourself" in a resumé, what points would you make?

K. Proverbs and Sayings

Ask Americans to explain these proverbs and sayings to you. Then ask them for other examples of sayings about competition, winning, or success.

1. When the going gets tough, the tough get going.
2. Every man for himself.
3. May the best man win.
4. To the winner belong the spoils.
5. It's a dog-eat-dog world.
6. Take care of number 1.

L. Watch for This

Edward T. Hall has described two basic types of cultures, with regard to the ways those cultures deal with time. He calls these "monochronic" and "polychronic" cultures. In monochronic cultures people do "one thing at a time." In polychronic cultures people do "many things at a time." For example, in a monochronic culture, when someone has a business appointment, that person expects to have the complete attention of the other party until the appointment has ended. On the other hand, in a polychronic culture, a person who has a business appointment expects there to be many others waiting and being dealt with at one time.

* This article is available from "Power of the Printed Word," International Paper Company, Dept. 10V, P. O. Box 954, Madison Square Station, N.Y., N.Y. 10010.

Which of the labels best describes activities and the way they are scheduled in your country? Which best describes the United States? Which would best describe the following situations:

1. You arrive at the airport an hour before your flight to find that there are large crowds pushing their way to the counter. Whoever pushes hardest, gets to the front and gets waited on. The ticket agent behind the counter serves several people at once, focusing attention on the one who has made himself or herself most noticed.
2. The doctor has told you that he will meet you at the hospital at 10:00 a.m. to take care of a minor problem. You have difficulty finding transportation, but finally arrive at 10:45. The doctor is seeing another patient and sends word that he will not be able to see you now until he can "squeeze you in" around his other appointments. You will probably have to wait until late afternoon.

Newark Airport. *Marc Anderson.*

M. Suggestions for Further Reading

Theodore Dreiser. *An American Tragedy.*
Horatio Alger. *Ragged Dick* and *Mark, the Match Boy.*
Arthur Miller. *Death of a Salesman.*
F. Scott Fitzgerald. "The Diamond as Big as the Ritz".
Sloan Wilson. *The Man in the Gray Flannel Suit.*
Ralph Nader. *Unsafe at Any Speed.*
Sinclair Lewis. *Babbitt.*
William H. Whyte, Jr. *The Organization Man.*

The United States Capitol Building: the meeting place for Congress.

chapter 7

Government and Politics in the United States

A wise and frugal Government shall restrain men from injuring one another, shall leave them otherwise free to regulate their own pursuits of industry and improvements.

Thomas Jefferson

A woman who has lived in the United States for many years was explaining why it was difficult for her parents and sister to come to visit her in the United States. Because her government wishes to discourage people from traveling abroad and spending their money in other countries, the Minister of Finance decided to require tourists leaving the country to deposit $1,200 in a special account before leaving the country. Whey they return, the money is refunded, with no interest paid on it. This was the decision of the Minister of Finance and the President, she said, and the Congress was not even consulted. "What happens if Congress disagrees with the President?" her American friend asked. "Oh," she replied, "the President can just tell the Congress to take a vacation, and then he can go on and pass new laws or do whatever he wants." The American was surprised. "Do you mean that the President can close the Congress if he wishes?" "Yes," she said, "and this has happened several times. The executive branch has much more power in our country than it does in the United States."

A Suspicion of Strong Government

The ideal of the free individual has had a profound effect on the way Americans view their government. There is deep suspicion that government is the natural enemy of freedom, even if it is elected by the people. The bigger and stronger the government is, the more dangerous to individual freedom Americans believe it to be.

Therefore, Americans tend to believe that government can safely serve only one purpose: to create conditions favorable to the protection of the freedom of the individual. They generally are strongly opposed to the view that government ought to have a collective purpose, such as the achievement of national glory or the establishment of a socialist society. Such high-sounding political slogans are viewed with suspicion. Politicians who say that government should play such a collective role may really want to take away individual freedom. These politicians may really be trying to acquire more power for themselves as leaders.

This suspicion of strong government goes back to the men who led the American Revolution in 1776. These men believed the government of Great Britain was determined to discourage the freedom and economic opportunities of the American colonists by excessive taxes and other measures which would ultimately benefit the British aristocracy and monarchy. Thomas Paine, the famous revolutionary writer, expressed the view of other American revolutionists when he said, "Government even in its best state is but a necessary evil; in its worst state, an **intolerable** one."

The signing of the Declaration of Independence, July 4, 1776. *National Archives.*

The Organization of the American Government

The way in which the national government is organized in the United States Constitution provides an excellent illustration of the American suspicion of governmental power. The provisions of the Constitution are more concerned with keeping the government from doing evil than with enabling it to do good. The national government, for example, is divided into three separate branches. This division of governmental power is based on the belief that if any one part or branch of government has all, or even most of the power, it will become a threat to the freedom of individual citizens.

The legislative or lawmaking branch of the government is called the Congress. The President, or Chief Executive, heads the second or executive branch, which has responsibility to carry out the law. The Supreme Court and lower national courts make up the third or **judicial** branch. The judicial branch settles disputes about the exact meaning of the law through court cases.

If any one of the three branches starts to **abuse** its power, the other two may join together against it to stop it. The Constitution is most careful in balancing the powers of the legislative and executive branches of the government because these two (Congress and the President) are the most powerful of the three branches. In almost every important area of governmental activity such as the power to make laws, the power to make war, or the power to conclude treaties with foreign countries, the Constitution gives each of these two branches enough power to prevent the other from acting on its own power alone.

The President and Congress have almost complete political independence from each other because they are both chosen in separate elections. For example, the election of the Congress does not determine who will be elected President, and the Presidential election does not determine who will be elected to Congress. It is quite possible in the American system to have the leader of one political party win the Presidency while the other major political party wins most of the seats in Congress.

Observers from other countries are often confused by the American system. The national government often seems to speak with two conflicting voices, that of the President and that of Congress. It is necessary for the President to sign bills passed by Congress in order for them to become law. A legislative bill passed by Congress dies if the President **vetoes** it, that is, if he refuses to sign it. On the other hand, a treaty with a foreign government signed by the President dies if Congress refuses to **ratify** it. It is necessary for the Senate to ratify such treaties by voting to accept them.

Although the American system of divided governmental power strikes many observers as inefficient and even disorganized, most Americans still strongly believe in it for two reasons: (1) it has been able to meet the challenges of the past, and (2) it gives strong protection to individual freedoms.

In addition to dividing government powers into three branches, the Constitution includes a "Bill of Rights" which is designed to protect specific individual rights and freedoms from government interference. Some of the guarantees in the Bill of Rights concern the freedom of expression. The government may not

The White House: the official home of the President of the United States, in Washington, D.C. *Marc Anderson.*

interfere with an individual's freedom of speech or freedom of religious worship. The Bill of Rights also guarantees the right of a fair criminal procedure for those accused of breaking laws. Thus, the Bill of Rights is another statement of the American belief in the importance of individual freedom.

The Ideal of the Free Individual

In the late 1700s most Americans expected the new national government created by the Constitution to leave them alone to pursue their individual goals. They believed the central purpose of government was to create the conditions most favorable to the development of the free individual.

Before the Civil War of the 1860s the American ideal of the free individual was the frontiersman and the small farmer. President Thomas Jefferson expressed this ideal when he said: "Those who labor in the earth are the chosen people of God, if ever he had a chosen people . . . ." Jefferson glorified the farmer for being a free individual who relied on no one but himself for his daily needs. Being dependent on none but himself, the farmer, he believed, was the most honest of citizens. Throughout his life Jefferson favored a small, weak form of government, which he believed would encourage the development of a nation of free, self-reliant farmer citizens.

From the end of the Civil War until the Great Depression of the 1930s the successful businessman replaced the farmer and the frontiersman as the ideal expression of the free individual. The prevailing view of Americans during this time was that government should not interfere in the activities of businessmen. If it were to do so, it would threaten the development of free individuals whose competitive spirit, self-reliance, and hard work were developing the United States into a land of greater and greater material prosperity.

Government, therefore, remained small and inactive in relation to the great size of the nation and the amount of power of business corporations. There were some government regulations over business during this period, but these had only a small impact on business practices. From the 1870s until the 1930s business organizations and ideas dominated American government and politics. The Republican party, one of the nation's two major political parties, provided the means for maintaining this dominance. The Republicans were more successful than their rivals, the Democrats, in electing Presidents and Congressmen during this period, and the Republicans strongly supported government policies favorable to business.

The Development of Big Government: The Welfare State

As we have seen in the previous chapter, the Great Depression of the 1930s greatly weakened the businessman's position as the American ideal of the free individual. The Depression also created the need for emergency government action to help the needy on a scale never before seen in peacetime. As a result of the Great Depression, the idea that government should be small and inactive was largely abandoned. Moreover, the ideal of the free individual underwent some very important changes.

The widespread unemployment and other economic hardships of the Depression gave rise to the new **assumption** that individuals could not be expected to rely on themselves alone in providing for their economic security. This new assumption, in turn, led to a large and active role for the national government in helping individuals meet their daily needs. The Democratic party, led by President Franklin Roosevelt, brought about a number of changes in the 1930s, which he referred to as a "New Deal" for Americans.

Even with the return of prosperity after the Depression and World War II (1941-1945), the growth of government's role in helping to provide economic security for individuals did not end. It continued in the prosperous postwar years. Roosevelt's New Deal had given birth to a permanent "welfare state" which provided government payments for retired persons over 65, payments for the unemployed, payments to families with dependent children and no father to provide income, and a number of other benefits for needy persons.

Although the welfare state grew rapidly in the decades after World War II, it has never been fully accepted by most Americans. Americans fear that economic

Franklin D. Roosevelt, President of the United States 1933-1945. *Library of Congress.*

security provided by the government will weaken self-reliance, an ideal that is closely associated in the minds of Americans with individual freedom.

Most Americans believe that although the welfare state began with good intentions, it is at best a necessary evil. At worst, it presents a danger to individual freedom by making an increasing number of Americans dependent on the government instead of on themselves. In this way, the strong traditions of individualism and self-reliance have made Americans less accepting of welfare state programs than the citizens of other democracies such as those in Western Europe which have more extensive welfare programs than those of the United States.

The welfare state in the United States has also been troubled by racial problems, which began with black slavery before the Civil War of the 1860s and continued with racial **segregation** in the South until the 1960s. Segregation made it difficult for black Americans to become **assimilated** into the larger middle-class culture and its values. Although American blacks made significant gains in the 1960s, millions are still unable to escape from poverty and unemployment. For this reason, a large number of people who receive welfare benefits are black Americans. Many racial prejudices against black Americans have been transferred to welfare programs.

Welfare programs are strongly disliked by most Americans because they go against the basic value of self-reliance. Most Americans believe that having to "go on welfare" in order to meet their daily needs is a personal embarrassment and a mark of failure. Even people who have been supported by welfare payments for much of their lives complain that the system is **degrading** and causes them to lose self-respect.

The Role of Special Interest Groups

The great expansion of governmental activity over the last 50 years is only partly due to the growth of welfare programs which help the poor and the needy. Practically all social and economic classes of Americans have seen the need to take advantage of, and to protect themselves from, the actions of government, especially the national government. To accomplish this, Americans with similar interests have formed special interest groups to more effectively influence the actions of government. These special interest groups are often called **lobbying** groups or "pressure" groups.

Although lobbying groups have existed throughout the nation's history, they have grown and prospered in the decades following the New Deal and World War II. By 1980, when there were more than 15,000 lobbyists in the nation's capital, one of the leaders in Congress exclaimed: "Everybody in America has a lobby."

The National Rifle Association (mentioned in Chapter 4) is an example of a powerful and effective lobby. Its members are mostly people who own guns for hunting and personal protection. The NRA, however, receives a great deal of money from business corporations that manufacture guns. Because of the attitudes and interests of its members, the NRA strongly opposes almost all government **restrictions** on the sale of both handguns and rifles. Even though most of the general public favors stronger gun controls, the NRA has prevented the government from taking such action.

Although few interest groups have been as successful as the NRA, most well-organized interest groups have achieved a large measure of success. By organizing into groups which put pressure on government officials, people can gain more rewards and avoid more government restrictions than if they tried to do it as individuals.

With this principle in mind, business interest groups have multiplied in recent decades so that almost every major trade or business has its lobbyists in Washington. Labor unions, which were made strong during the New Deal years, have their influential lobbyists. So do farm groups. Interest groups representing ethnic groups such as black Americans, American Indians, Mexican Americans, and Jewish Americans have also expanded. There are interest groups representing a variety of ideals or causes which want government support. These include equal rights for women, a clean environment, and greater protection for consumers. Even the people who receive welfare payments have a lobbying group called the Welfare Rights Organization.

John F. Kennedy seeking the support of a labor union in his 1960 campaign to become President. *AFL-CIO News.*

The political tendency of recent decades is for the size of the government to bring about an increase in the number and size of interest groups, and for the greater demands made on the government by interest groups to increase the size of the government. The result of this continuing cycle can be referred to as interest group government. No single interest dominates government and politics as business groups did before the Great Depression. Rather, government and politics are based on reaching compromises with a larger number of groups and pleasing as many as possible.

The New Individualism Versus the Old Individualism

Interest group government can be seen as expressing a new form of American individualism. Unlike the case with frontier individualism or business individualism, individuals do not claim to succeed on their own, but rather by forming groups to influence the government. Still, it is individuals, their rights, their interests, and their ambitions, not those of the group, that are the focus of attention. The interest group is no more than a tool to achieve the goals of the individual by influencing the government.

The Democratic party emerged from the New Deal as the sponsor and supporter of the welfare state and interest group government. The Republicans continued to base their doctrines on the older individualism drawn from the period of business dominance before the Great Depression.

As the decade of the 1980s began, many observers expressed the view that neither the Republican idea of national prosperity through business dominance nor the Democratic idea of national prosperity through the welfare state and interest group government was adequate to meet the common problems and common dangers facing Americans in the closing decades of the twentieth century.

The political parties, however, merely reflected the historic American tradition of defining the common good of the nation, as well as the purpose of government, in terms of the welfare and freedom of the individual. The weakness of this political tradition may be that it gives almost no support to the idea of the common good of the nation, which requires the willing sacrifice of the self-interest of the individual. In the twentieth century, however, Americans saw military dictatorships rise to power in other countries because too little importance was placed on the individual. This helped to reassure them that their approach to politics and government was sound. Nevertheless, it is likely that Americans will have to move beyond the individualism of business ideas and of interest group government if they are to deal effectively with the serious problems which affect them all.

New Words

intolerable that which cannot be allowed; unbearable

judicial having to do with a court of law

abuse to use in a wrong way

veto to refuse to allow, to forbid

ratify to approve an agreement and make it official

assumption something that is believed to be true

segregation the separation of one social or racial group from another

assimilate to become part of a group

degrade to lower in the opinion of others

lobby a group of people who unite for or against an action so that those in power will change their minds

restriction a limitation, control, or regulation

A. Vocabulary Practice

Match the word with its definition.

____ 1. abuse	a. to become part of a group
____ 2. assimilate	b. a limitation or regulation
____ 3. assumption	c. what the Senate has to do to make a treaty official
____ 4. intolerable	d. the branch of government that has the courts of law
____ 5. judicial	e. what the President does to a bill to prevent it from becoming law
____ 6. lobby	f. a pressure group which tries to influence government
____ 7. ratify	g. unbearable
____ 8. restriction	h. to use power in a wrong way
____ 9. segregation	i. the separation of black people and white people into separate groups
____ 10. veto	j. something believed to be true

B. Comprehension Check

Write the letter of the best answer according to the information in the chapter.

____ 1. Americans do not want to have a strong national government because
   a. they are afraid of their political leaders.
   b. they are afraid it will put limits on their individual freedom.
   c. they are much more concerned with national glory.

____ 2. The Constitution of the United States
   a. gives by far the most power to Congress.
   b. gives by far the most power to the President.
   c. tries to give each branch enough power to balance the others.

____ 3. The President of the United States
   a. has the power to make official treaties with foreign governments without the approval of Congress.
   b. can veto a law that has been passed by Congress.
   c. is elected if his political party wins most of the seats in Congress.

____ 4. The Bill of Rights
   a. explains the rights of Congress and the rights of the President.
   b. guarantees citizens of the United States specific individual rights and freedoms.
   c. is part of the Declaration of Independence.

____ 5. The American ideal of the free individual
   a. was exemplified by the farmers and the frontiersmen in the late 1700s and early 1800s.

b. was exemplified by the businessman before the Civil War of the 1860s.
c. caused the national government to grow in size and strength during the late 1800s.

____ 6. The size and power of the United States government
a. have remained the same since the nation began in the late 1700s.
b. have decreased greatly since the Great Depression of the 1930s.
c. have increased greatly since the Great Depression of the 1930s.

____ 7. The welfare state
a. was created during a time of great economic prosperity.
b. started with President Roosevelt's New Deal.
c. is based on the idea that all individuals should be self-reliant and responsible for their own welfare.

____ 8. Stronger gun control laws are favored by
a. the National Rifle Association.
b. most of the American people.
c. very few Americans.

____ 9. Lobbying groups are formed mainly to
a. influence the government.
b. influence public opinion.
c. provide information of interest to their members.

____ 10. Special interest groups have
a. caused the government to get larger.
b. caused the government to get smaller.
c. had little influence on the size of government.

C. Questions for Discussion and Composition

1. What makes Americans suspicious of a strong government? Basically, what do they think the role of government should be? How do people in your country view the role of the government in your society?
2. How is the government of your country organized? Is there a monarchy? Do you have a president? A prime minister? How are the leaders of your country chosen? Does the party that wins the most seats in the legislature choose the president (or prime minister)?
3. What happened in the 1930s which caused the United States government to suddenly grow much larger and more powerful? How has your government responded to economic crises? Does a government have a responsibility to provide welfare programs for its needy people?
4. What is a lobby group? What kind of special interest groups are there in the United States? Are there similar lobbies in your country? If so, are they effective in influencing government officials?

5. What is the National Rifle Association? Why has the NRA stopped gun control legislation in the United States? How do the majority of Americans feel about gun control? Could this happen in your country?
6. What is the difference between the "new" individualism and the "old" individualism? In your opinion, which is more important, the rights of individuals or the good of the nation as a whole?

D. Cloze Summary Paragraph

This paragraph summarizes the chapter. Fill in each blank with any word that makes sense.

Americans believe that the ____*role*____ of their government is ________ protect their individual freedom. ________ Constitution divides the powers ________ the government among the ________ branches: the executive, the ________ and the judicial. This ________ any branch from gaining ________ much power and threatening ________. Because the ideal of ________ free individual was so ________, for many years the ________ remained small and weak, ________ individuals to pursue their ________ goals. In the 1930s, ________, there was an economic ________ and the role of ________ changed. Welfare programs were ________ to help the needy ________ the government grew much ________ and stronger. Also, many ________ groups were established to ________ the government. These special ________ groups represent the desires ________ the individuals in the ________. Although most Americans have ________ in some way from ________ government programs, the majority

__________ them are still suspicious __________ the power of big __________. They are more concerned __________ their individual freedom than __________ are with the common __________ of the country.

E. Ask Americans

Find out how Americans feel about their government by asking a number of them the question below. Compare their responses with the poll which follows.

I'm going to read you a list of areas in which government might play a role. For each, please tell me if you think the government should play a major role, a minor role, or no role at all.

1. Seeing to it that all Americans get good health care
2. Protecting the environment
3. Encouraging economic development
4. Seeing to it that there are enough good jobs
5. Fostering basic research
6. Helping American business compete with foreign business
7. Increasing the number of blacks and minorities in good jobs
8. Fostering the arts

OPINION ROUNDUP

MAJOR ROLE FOR GOVERNMENT SEEN

Question: I'm going to read you a list of areas in which government might play a role. For each, please tell me if you think the government should play a major role, a minor role, or no role at all. First, increasing the number of blacks and minorities in good jobs. (Ask about each item)

Government should play a major role in...	Major role	Minor role	No role	Don't know
Seeing to it that all Americans get good health care	73%	20%	5%	2%
Protecting the environment	72%	23%	3%	2%
Encouraging economic development	70%	23%	4%	3%
Seeing to it that there are enough good jobs	63%	25%	9%	2%
Fostering basic research	56%	33%	6%	5%
Helping American business compete with foreign business	55%	27%	14%	4%
Increasing the number of blacks and minorities in good jobs	33%	34%	31%	3%
Fostering the arts	20%	46%	27%	7%

Source: Survey by the Roper Organization/Roper Center for Public Opinion Research for the American Enterprise Institute, November 14-21, 1981.

Public Opinion, February/March 1982

F. Outlining

The following outline of the chapter is a sentence outline. The main ideas are all there, but some of the supporting details have been omitted. Skim the chapter to find the missing information and fill in the blanks to complete the outline. Be sure that each entry is a *complete sentence* and *not* an incomplete phrase.

Introduction: The rights of individual citizens are central to the American view of government.

I. Most Americans are suspicious of a strong government.
   A. They are afraid that government may interfere with their freedom.
      1. The bigger the government is, the greater the danger.
      2. Americans would rather have their government protect individual freedom than work on some collective goal.
   B. The suspicion of strong government goes back to the time of the American Revolution.
      1. People believed that the British government was more interested in collecting taxes than protecting the freedom and economic interest of the colonists.
      2. The leaders of the Revolution wanted their government to have as little power as possible.

II. The American government is organized to keep it from being too powerful.
   A. The power of the government is divided among three separate branches.
      1. The legislative branch (Congress) makes the laws.
      2. ______________________________
      3. ______________________________
   B. The branches each have separate powers that balance each other and keep any one branch from becoming too powerful.
      1. Members of Congress and the President are chosen in separate elections.
      2. The President may veto bills passed by Congress.
      3. ______________________________
   C. Individual freedom is also protected in the Bill of Rights.
      1. ______________________________
      2. ______________________________

III. The American ideal of the free individual has discouraged the development of a strong government.
   A. Before the Civil War, the farmer and the frontiersman exemplified the ideal of the free individual.
      1. ______________________________
      2. ______________________________

B. From the end of the Civil War until the Great Depression of the 1930s, the businessman exemplified the ideal of the free individual.
1. ______
2. ______

IV. In the 1930s the government began to grow in size and strength, and the welfare state was born.
A. The Great Depression created the need for government help for the needy.
1. ______
2. ______
B. The welfare state continued to grow after the economic crisis had passed.
1. ______
2. ______
C. Americans have never fully accepted their welfare state.
1. ______
2. ______
3. ______

V. In the decades following World War II special interest groups have played an important role in American government.
A. Americans have formed lobbying groups.
1. ______
2. ______
B. The NRA is an example of a powerful lobby.
1. ______
2. ______
C. Lobbying groups represent a wide range of interests.
1. ______
2. ______
3. ______
D. The existence of powerful special interest groups has an effect on the size of the government.
1. ______
2. ______

VI. There is a new form of individualism in American government.
A. Interest group government and the welfare state represent the new individualism.
1. ______
2. ______
B. Neither the old nor the new individualism supports the idea of individual sacrifice for the common good.
1. ______
2. ______

Conclusion: It will be necessary to move beyond both forms of individualism for the government to solve the country's problems.

G. Ask Yourself

Which of the following things do you think your government should pay for?

1. Free medical care for all citizens
2. Free education for all citizens
3. Basic food and housing for all citizens
4. Highways, roads, water systems, and other public works
5. Complete care for the elderly
6. Complete care for needy children
7. Public transportation (trains, buses)

Which of these does your government now pay for?

(2) (4) (6)

H. Suggestions for Research

1. You may be surprised to learn that the President of the United States is not elected directly by the people, but by the Electoral College. In Presidential elections people are actually voting for the "electors," and it is these electors who officially choose the President.

   With the Electoral College system, the winner of the majority of each state's popular votes gets all of that state's electoral votes. Though the number of electoral votes varies according to population, it is possible for a person to be elected President without carrying a majority of the popular (individual) votes. That happened in 1888, when Benjamin Harrison won the Presidency even though Grover Cleveland had the majority of popular votes.

   Look in an encyclopedia for an explanation of the Electoral College and its role in elections. At the time of a Presidential election you will see many articles about the Electoral College in newspapers and news magazines. How do Americans feel about this system?

2. Review the Bill of Rights and then decide if each of the following laws would be "unconstitutional" or not. What article of the Bill of Rights deals with each?
   a. You cannot hold a meeting to discuss corruption in government.
   b. A major city newspaper is prevented from reporting about the political activities of a member of the President's Cabinet.
   c. Your family is prevented from worshipping at a church that is new and is believed to be "strange."
   d. If you disagree with the President, you cannot legally say so in public.

3. Americans believe that religion and government should be kept separate (the separation of church and state). However, there are many who believe that the

United States government is influenced by Christianity. Do you agree? What examples do you find of that? Consider the following and ask Americans for their opinions.

a. Consider the American workweek. What day is a "holiday"?
b. Consider what holidays are national. Are any of these Christian?

4. In the United States there are an estimated 60 million handguns in circulation, one for every four people. Murders by handguns occur at the rate of one per 10,000 people each year. Find out about gun control laws in other countries, the number of guns owned by individuals, and the yearly murder rate.

I. Suggestions for Writing

1. In 1981 the President shocked the American public by vetoing a bill that would pay federal government employees. As a result, most government employees were sent home, since they could no longer be paid for their work. Could this happen in your country? Which branches of government were competing for power in this case? What is your feeling about sending most of the government employees home?

2. Sandra Day O'Connor became the first female Supreme Court Justice when she was appointed in 1981. Why do you think a woman was appointed to the Supreme Court? What principles of American life does her appointment reflect?

3. It has been said that everyone in the United States has a lobby. Below is a list of only a few of the many groups representing special interests of Americans. Do you share any of these interests? Would you want to belong to any of these groups? Choose a group and explain why you believe it should be heard by the government.

Conservation or environmental protection groups
Handgun control or pro-gun (gun lobby) groups
Unions
Professional associations (doctors, lawyers, teachers, etc.)
Pro- or anti-nuclear groups
Veterans' groups
Women's groups
Ethnic associations
Health groups
Pro- or anti-abortion groups
"Operation Rescue" (=) Anti-abortion groups -
Gay rights groups
Groups for or against prayer in the public schools

J. Ask Americans about Political Labels

Being Republican or Democratic is becoming less important in American politics. Instead, a number of voters look to see which candidate is "liberal" and which is "conservative." The Republican party has been growing increasingly conservative or "right wing," while the Democratic party is increasingly considered liberal or "left wing." Many Americans consider themselves neither conservative nor liberal: they call themselves "middle of the roaders" or "moderates."

What do you think the positions of liberals and conservatives would be on the following issues?

1. Control of handguns
2. Sale of pornography
3. Guaranteed jobs and housing for everyone
4. Sex education courses
5. Legalization of marijuana
6. Government support (financial) for abortions

Ask several Americans whether they are opposed to or in favor of each of the above. Then ask them whether they are liberals or conservatives.

K. People Watching

Americans sometimes say that it is dangerous to talk about two topics: religion and politics. It's often difficult to know what you should say to people when you first meet them. The questions you might ask others from your country may not be appropriate or acceptable in another society or culture.

Ask a number of Americans of different ages, of both sexes, and of different ethnic or racial backgrounds, if possible, the following questions. Record each person's reaction to each question. Write down not only what someone said, but also how that person behaved. Did the person look surprised? Shocked? Embarrassed? What did the person do? Did the person look away? Did the person look down?

After you have finished asking the questions, ask each person whether there were any questions which that person felt should not be asked and why. Write your findings. Which questions are acceptable? Which are unacceptable? Which are acceptable in your country?

1. What is your name?
2. What do you do for a living?
3. Where are you from? (or, Where do you live?)

4. Do you like your job?
5. How much do you make?
6. Are you a Republican or a Democrat? Why?
7. Are you married? Why or why not?
8. Do you have children? Why or why not?
9. How old are you?
10. What is your religion?

Bill Jackson.

L. Suggestions for Further Reading

Frank Norris. *The Octopus.*
Robert Penn Warren. *All the King's Men.*
James Agee. *Let Us Now Praise Famous Men.*

Irish Americans march in St. Patrick's Day Parade. *Marc Anderson.*

chapter 8

Ethnic and Racial Assimilation in the United States

So in this continent, the energy of Irish, Germans, Swedes, Poles and all the European tribes, of the Africans, and of the Polynesians—will construct a new race, a new religion, a new state.

Ralph Waldo Emerson

A man who is now a citizen of the United States was describing his escape to several American friends. He had been a musician in the state orchestra and was on tour in America when he decided to stay. "It was something I had planned for many years," he explained. "Life had become unbearable and I had friends in Japan and in many European countries. There were several countries where I could have been very happy and had opportunities to play in orchestras."

"Then why did you choose the United States?" his American friend asked. "Oh," he said, "because in America, everyone came from another country. Here I fit in—I can be an American and not a foreigner."

Melting Pot or Salad Bowl

The population of the United States includes a large variety of ethnic groups coming from many races, nationalities, and religions. The process by which these many groups have been made a part of a common cultural life with commonly shared values is called "assimilation." Scholars disagree as to the extent to which assimilation has occurred in the United States. Some have described the United States as a "melting pot" where various racial and ethnic groups have been combined into one culture. Others are inclined to see the United States as a "salad bowl" where the various groups have remained distinct and different from one another while living in the same country.

The truth probably lies between these two views. An enormous amount of racial and ethnic assimilation has taken place in the United States, yet some groups continue to feel a strong sense of separateness from the culture as a whole.

Generally speaking, whites from different national and religious backgrounds have been largely assimilated into the larger American culture. American Jews are the only group of whites who retain a strong sense of separateness from the larger culture. This results from a long history of persecution in the Christian countries in Europe, the weaker forms of **discrimination** and anti-Jewish feeling that exist in the United States, and their own strong feeling of ethnic pride. Yet along with their sense of separateness, at the same time American Jews have a strong sense of being a part of the larger American culture in which they have achieved competitive success in almost every field. Therefore, unlike other groups of white Americans, the Jews have a feeling of being separate that remains as strong as the feeling of being assimilated into the larger American culture.

The Establishment of the Dominant Culture

The process of assimilating a large number of white ethnic groups into American life did present problems. At the time of the American Revolution the population was largely English in origin, Protestant, and middle class. These characteristics became the standard for judging other groups. Those having a different religion such as the Irish Catholics or those speaking a different language such as the Germans, Dutch, and Swedes, were in the minority and would be disadvantaged unless they became assimilated. In the late 1700s this assimilation occurred without great difficulty. According to two historians, "English, Irish, German,... Dutch, Swedish—**mingled** and intermarried with little thought of any difference."*

The dominant American culture, therefore, grew out of the nation's early history. It was English-speaking, Western European, Protestant, and middle class in character. The assumption was made that immigrants having these characteristics would give the strongest support to the basic values of the culture such as freedom, equality of opportunity, and the desire to work hard for a higher material standard of living.

* Allan Nevins and Henry Steele Commager, *America: The Story of a Free People* (Boston: Little, Brown and Co., 1942), p. 58.

The Assimilation of Non-Protestant and Non-Western Europeans

As is the case in many cultures, the degree to which a minority group was seen as different from the characteristics of the dominant majority determined the extent of that group's acceptance. Immigrants who were like the earlier settlers were accepted. The large numbers of immigrants with significantly different characteristics tended to be viewed as a threat to basic American values and the American way of life.

This was particularly true of the immigrants who arrived by the millions during the late nineteenth and early twentieth centuries. Most of them came from poverty-stricken nations of southern and eastern Europe. They spoke languages other than English, and large numbers of them were Catholics or Jews.

Americans at the time were very fearful of this new flood of immigrants. They were afraid that these people were so accustomed to lives of poverty and dependence that they would not understand such basic American values as freedom, self-reliance, and competition. There were so many new immigrants that they might even change the basic values of the nation in undesirable ways.

Americans tried to meet what they saw as a threat to their values by offering English instruction for the new immigrants and citizenship classes to teach them basic American beliefs. The immigrants, however, often felt that their American teachers disapproved of the traditions of their homeland. Moreover, learning about American values gave them little help in meeting their most important needs such as employment, food, and a place to live.

Mulberry Street, in the heart of the immigrant area of New York City in the early 1900s. *Library of Congress.*

Far more helpful to the new immigrants were the "political bosses" of the larger cities of the northeastern United States, where most of the immigrants first arrived. Those bosses saw to many of the practical needs of the immigrants and were more accepting of the different homeland traditions. In exchange for their help, the political bosses expected the immigrants to keep them in power by voting for them in elections.

Many Americans strongly disapproved of the political bosses. This was partly because the bosses were frequently **corrupt**; that is, they often stole money from the city governments they controlled and engaged in other illegal practices. Perhaps more important to disapproving native Americans, however, was the fact that the bosses seemed to be destroying such basic American values as self-reliance and competition.

The bosses, it seemed, were teaching the immigrants to be dependent on them rather than to rely on themselves. Moreover, the bosses were "buying" the votes of the immigrants in order to give themselves a monopoly of political power in many large cities. This practice destroyed competition for political office, which Americans viewed as an important tradition in politics just as it was in other facets of American life.

Despite these criticisms, many scholars believe that the political bosses performed an important function in the late nineteenth and early twentieth centuries. They helped to assimilate large numbers of disadvantaged white immigrants into the larger American culture. The bosses helped the first generation of immigrants to get a start in a strange new land. The bosses also helped the sons and daughters of these immigrants find jobs. The second generation, of course, had the advantage of learning English as their native language.

The fact that the United States had a rapidly expanding economy at the turn of the century made it possible for these new immigrants, often with the help of the bosses, to better their standard of living in the United States. As a result of these new opportunities and new rewards, immigrants came to accept most of the values of the larger American culture and were in turn accepted by the great majority of Americans. For white ethnic groups, therefore, it is generally true that their feeling of being a part of the larger culture—that is, "American"—is much stronger than their feeling of belonging to a separate ethnic group—Irish, Italian, Polish, etc.

The Assimilation of Non-European Groups

The process of assimilation in the United States has been much more successful for white ethnic groups than for nonwhite ethnic groups. Of the nonwhite ethnic groups, Americans of African descent—"black" Americans—have had the greatest difficulty in becoming assimilated into the larger culture. Blacks alone were brought to the United States against their will to be sold as slaves. Except for the native American Indian tribes who inhabited the United States before the first white settlers arrived, all other ethnic groups came to the United States voluntarily as immigrants in order to better their living conditions.

The enslavement of blacks in the United States was a complete contradiction of such basic American values as freedom and equality of opportunity. It divided the United States into two increasingly different sections: the southern states, in which black slavery became the basis of society, and the northern states, which did not allow slavery.

A minority of whites in the North insisted that slavery and freedom could not exist together in a free country and demanded that slavery be abolished even if this meant war with the South. A much larger number of northern whites believed that freedom and equality of opportunity needed to be protected for the white man only, but they were afraid that black slavery would eventually take away their freedoms. If, for example, the slave system of the South were allowed to spread into the frontier regions of the West, the white man's freedom would be in danger. Poor and middle-income whites could no longer look to the western frontier as a land of equality and opportunity where a man could better his position in life. Rather, men would have to compete with unpaid slave labor, a situation that would degrade their work and lower their social status.

Abraham Lincoln was able to become President of the United States by appealing to both the white idealists who saw slavery as an injustice to the black man and to the larger numbers of northern whites who saw slavery as a threat to themselves. Lincoln's argument was that if black slavery continued to spread

Lincoln's address at Gettysburg, Pennsylvania, November 19, 1863. *New York Public Library Picture Collection.*

westward, the white man's freedom and equality would be threatened. Lincoln also believed that basic ideals such as freedom and equality of opportunity had to apply to *all* men, black and white, or they would not last as basic American values.

When Lincoln won the Presidency in 1860, the southern states left the Union and tried to form a new nation of their own based on slavery. A Civil War between the North and South resulted, which turned out to be the bloodiest and most destructive of all the nation's wars. When the North was finally victorious, black slavery ended in the United States.

However, blacks were not readily assimilated into the larger American culture. Most remained in the South, where they were not allowed to vote and were legally segregated from whites in a manner very similar to South Africa's **apartheid** system. Moreover, blacks continued to be the **victims** of strong racial prejudice in both the North and the South.

This state of affairs remained unchanged until the U.S. Supreme Court declared in 1954 that racially segregated public schools did not provide equal educational opportunities for black Americans and were therefore illegal. Black leaders throughout the United States were greatly encouraged by this decision. They decided to try to end racial segregation in all areas of American life.

The most important of these leaders was Martin Luther King, Jr., a black Protestant minister with a great gift for **inspiring** his people. From the late 1950s until his **assassination** by a white gunman in 1968, King led thousands of black people in nonviolent marches and demonstrations against segregation and other forms of racial discrimination.

Martin Luther King, Jr.
The Bergen Record.

King's goal was to bring about greater assimilation of black people into the larger American culture. His ideals were largely developed from basic American values. He wanted greater equality of opportunity and "Freedom now" for his people. He did not wish to separate his people from American society, but rather to gain for them a larger part in it.

Some black leaders, such as Malcolm X, urged a rejection of basic American values and complete separation of blacks from the white culture. Malcolm X believed that American values were nothing more than "white man's values" used to keep blacks in an inferior position. Blacks must separate themselves from whites, by force if necessary, and build their own society based on values which they would create for themselves. The great majority of American blacks, however, shared Martin Luther King's beliefs and goals rather than those of Malcolm X, and looked to King as their leader.

Largely as a result of King's activities, two major **civil rights** laws were passed during the 1960s which removed racial segregation from public facilities in the South and also removed the **barriers** which had prevented black people from voting in that region.

The civil rights laws of the 1960s helped to bring about a significant degree of assimilation of blacks into the larger American culture. Most important, they helped to reduce the amount of white prejudice toward black people in all parts of the country. The number of blacks attending the nation's colleges and universities, holding elective public office, and earning higher incomes increased dramatically in the late 1960s and 1970s.

Nevertheless, the assimilation of blacks into American life has been only partly achieved. Significant differences remain between black and white earnings, black and white educational opportunities, and black and white social class standings. Therefore, black Americans are caught in a contradiction. Like white ethnic groups, they feel that they are part of the larger American culture. Unlike white ethnic groups, however, they also have a strong feeling of being separate from it.

To a somewhat lesser extent, these contradictory feelings are also held by other Americans such as Mexican Americans, Puerto Ricans, Asian Americans, and American Indians. These groups also have had to contend with the racial prejudices of the white majority, but not to the same extent as black Americans.

The Assimilation of Future Immigrants

The greatest problems of assimilation that lie ahead for the United States are probably those concerning black Americans and the rapidly growing Hispanic population of the United States. There are now approximately 8 million *Chicanos*, or Mexican Americans, in the United States. Thousands cross the Mexican border illegally each year to find jobs in the United States. Many other Latin Americans are also entering the country, handicapped by a lack of knowledge of the English language.

Chinatown, New York City. *N.Y. Convention & Visitors Bureau.*

At the beginning of the twentieth century the assimilation of white ethnic groups who were different in language, class, or religion from the majority was made possible in large part because the United States was a rapidly developing land of material abundance. Thus, new immigrants had the opportunity to better their condition and, in the process, to become attached to American ways and values. Assimilation will be more difficult during the rest of the twentieth century because the nation's economic growth and living standards have been declining, with no remedy as yet in sight.

Material abundance has been the life blood which has **sustained** Americans in their basic beliefs and values. As has been shown in this chapter, this has been true for the early settlers, the disadvantaged white immigrants, and, to a somewhat lesser extent, the descendants of black slaves as well. As the material abundance of the nation ceases to grow, the nation's capacity for assimilation, which has been great in the past, may decline. Every nation has its own limits as to how many different races, languages, religions, and nationalities it can assimilate and still function as one society. Only the future will tell for certain whether the United States, after three centuries of assimilation of diverse groups, is now approaching its own limits.

New Words

discrimination not treating all people the same, treating some differently
mingle to mix together
corrupt dishonest; immoral; bad
apartheid separating people by race; racial segregation
victim someone who suffers because of other people's actions
inspire to encourage in someone the ability to act
assassination the murder of a leader
civil rights rights such as freedom and equality which belong to citizens regardless of race, religion, sex, or other factors
barrier something placed in the way in order to prevent people from moving forward
sustain to keep strong

A. Vocabulary Check

Fill in the blank with the word from the vocabulary list that correctly completes the sentence.

1. In South Africa the system of separating the races is called ______.
2. Martin Luther King was able to ______ his followers to demonstrate against segregation.
3. Many of the big city political bosses were ______; they stole money from the city governments.
4. Jews have been the ______ of persecution in many countries.
5. People from many different countries who have come to the United States have ______ and many have married persons of a different national origin.
6. Martin Luther King was the most important black leader in America from the late 1950s until his ______ by a white gunman in 1968.
7. King and his followers tried to end racial ______ in the South; they believed everyone should be treated equally.
8. Black people in the 1950s and early 1960s did not have the same freedom and equality as whites in the South; they had to fight for their ______ ______.
9. Before black people could move forward, the ______ which had prevented them from voting had to be removed.
10. Material abundance has helped to ______ the American values and keep them strong.

B. Comprehension Check

Write the letter of the best answer according to the information in the chapter.

____ 1. Scholars who see the United States as a "salad bowl" emphasize
  a. the great extent of racial and ethnic assimilation in the United States.
  b. the many differences between racial and ethnic groups in the United States.
  c. the rapid growth of the population of the United States.

____ 2. Jews in American society feel that
  a. they are fully assimilated into American society.
  b. they do not belong at all to American society.
  c. they belong to American society, but at the same time they are separate from it.

____ 3. Which of the following was *not* a characteristic of American culture during the early decades of the nation's history?
  a. Catholic
  b. Western European
  c. middle class

____ 4. Which of the following was *true* about the political bosses in northeastern cities during the late nineteenth and early twentieth centuries?
  a. They were more afraid of new immigrants than were other Americans.
  b. They were more cruel to new immigrants than were other Americans.
  c. They were more helpful to new immigrants than were other Americans.

____ 5. Today ethnic groups in the United States
  a. have no feeling of belonging to an ethnic group (such as Irish, Italian, Polish) whatsoever.
  b. are assimilated into the dominant culture in varying degrees, depending on how similar their culture is to the majority.
  c. all feel much more a part of their ethnic group than a part of the dominant culture.

____ 6. What was the *main* reason northern whites disliked slavery?
  a. It went against their religious beliefs.
  b. It went against the U.S. Constitution.
  c. It threatened their own economic opportunities.

____ 7. After the Civil War black Americans in the South lived in a social system similar to
   a. South Africa's apartheid system.
   b. Europe's class system.
   c. Rome's slavery system.

____ 8. In 1954 the U.S. Supreme Court declared that black people in America
   a. could not be denied their right to vote for racial reasons.
   b. could not be forced to attend racially segregated public schools.
   c. could not be denied freedom of speech, press, or religion.

____ 9. On which of the beliefs listed below did Malcolm X *disagree* with Martin Luther King?
   a. Black people should be assimilated into the larger American society.
   b. Black people were not treated fairly by the larger American society.
   c. Black people must gain their freedom now, not in the distant future.

____ 10. Assimilation of many different ethnic and racial groups into the larger American society has been made possible *mainly* by
   a. the American belief in self-reliance.
   b. the respect all Americans have for hard work.
   c. the growth of material abundance in American society.

C. Questions for Discussion and Composition

1. This chapter describes the dominant American culture as being white, English-speaking, Protestant, and middle class. (This is sometimes called "WASP"—white, Anglo-Saxon, Protestant.) How would you describe the dominant culture of your country?
2. What ethnic groups in your country have significantly different characteristics from the dominant culture? How well are they assimilated into your society? Is your country more a "melting pot" or a "salad bowl"?
3. What is your country's policy on immigration? Is immigration encouraged or discouraged? Does your country permit "guest" workers? Are there language classes or government programs to help new immigrants assimilate? Do immigrants usually intermarry with natives of your country?
4. Are there any groups in your country that experience discrimination because of their family origin? Their national origin? Their race? Their religion? Are there any laws that either permit or forbid discrimination?
5. What is the official language of your country? Is there more than one official language? What other languages are spoken in your country? Do most people know more than one language? Does language separate groups in your country in any way?

D. Outlining

The following outline of the chapter is a topic outline. Change it into a sentence outline by rewriting each entry as a complete sentence. You will have to look at the chapter to find additional information in order to do this exercise. (At the end of the outline you will find that the first section has been done for you.)

Introduction: People of different races, nationalities, and religions

I. Melting pot or salad bowl
   A. Definition of melting pot
   B. Definition of salad bowl
   C. The separateness of American Jews
      1. The persecution experienced in Europe
      2. The weaker discrimination in the United States
      3. Their success in the United States

II. The establishment of the dominant culture
   A. The characteristics of the population at the time of the Revolution—English, Protestant, middle class
   B. The assimilation of people in the late 1700s
   C. The characteristics of the dominant culture today

III. The assimilation of non-Protestant and non-Western Europeans
   A. The immigrants of the late 1800s and early 1900s
      1. Where they came from
      2. How they were different
      3. How Americans viewed them
   B. The role of the big city political bosses in assimilation
      1. What the bosses did
      2. What the bosses expected in return
      3. Why Americans criticized the bosses
   C. The rapidly expanding economy
      1. The opportunities for new immigrants
      2. The acceptance of the new immigrants

IV. The assimilation of non-European groups
   A. The experience of black Americans
      1. Slavery in the South
      2. Why people in the North feared the spread of slavery
      3. The Civil War

B. The role of Martin Luther King
   1. Segregation in the South
   2. King's goal to end segregation and discrimination
   3. King's desire for complete assimilation of blacks into the American society

C. The civil rights laws of the 1960s
   1. An end to segregation
   2. A return of voting rights
   3. The position of blacks in society today

V. The assimilation of future immigrants
   A. Immigrants from Latin America
   B. The role of economic conditions
      1. An aid to assimilation in the past
      2. Future uncertainty about the economy and the ability to assimilate new immigrants

Conclusion: Uncertainty about future assimilation of new immigrants

An example of how to change the topic outline into a sentence outline is given below.

Introduction: The United States is made up of people of different races, nationalities and religions.

I. The United States has been described by some scholars as a melting pot and by others as a salad bowl.
   A. In a melting pot the racial and ethnic groups combine into one culture.
   B. In a salad bowl the groups remain distinct and different although they are mixed together.
   C. American Jews are the only groups of whites who retain a feeling of separateness.
      1. This is because of a history of persecution in Europe.
      2. Also, American Jews have experienced some discrimination in the United States.
      3. Jews have been very successful in the United States and are assimilated into the culture.

E. Cloze Summary Paragraph

This paragraph summarizes the chapter. Fill in each blank with any word that makes sense.

The people of the ___*United*___ States are from a ______________ variety of ethnic groups ______________ represent many races, nationalities, ______________ religions. Some of these ______________ have assimilated completely into ______________ main culture while others ______________ not. The more the ______________ differs from the characteristics ______________ the dominant culture—which ______________ white, English-speaking, Protestant, ______________ middle class—the less ______________ group is assimilated. In ______________ late 1800s and early ______________ large groups of Catholics ______________ Jews came from southern ______________ eastern European countries. Although ______________ were quite different from ______________ dominant American culture, they ______________ assimilated into the rapidly ______________ economy with the help ______________ big city political bosses. ______________ Americans have not assimilated ______________ as much success. Brought ______________ as slaves, they remained ______________ from whites in southern ______________ until Martin Luther King ______________ demonstrations against segregation and ______________ was ended in the ______________. In the future it ______________ become more difficult for ______________ United States to assimilate ______________ new groups as the ______________ material

abundance declines.

F. Ask Yourself

Do you agree or disagree with these statements?

1. I would emigrate to another country if I could have a better life there for myself and my family.	Agree	Disagree
2. Foreigners who come from any country in the world are welcomed in my country.	Agree	Disagree
3. My government should encourage refugees from other countries to settle in my country.	Agree	Disagree
4. My family would not object if I chose to marry someone of another nationality.	Agree	Disagree
5. My family would not object if I chose to marry someone of another race.	Agree	Disagree
6. It is important to maintain your own language and cultural traditions even if you have left your country.	Agree	Disagree
7. People are really basically the same all over the world.	Agree	Disagree
8. People who are very different from the dominant culture (race, religion, or ethnic background) have as high a status as anyone else in my country.	Agree	Disagree
9. Every person in the world should learn to speak at least one foreign language.	Agree	Disagree
10. I believe that my children will have a higher standard of living than I had growing up.	Agree	Disagree

G. Ask Americans

What should be the role of Americans in addressing past injustices to blacks? That is a major question still being debated by many Americans today. Americans need to decide whether minorities should be given preferential treatment in being admitted to college, in being hired or promoted on their jobs, and in other ways.

Ask several Americans the following questions.

1. Should black Americans receive special consideration in applying for admission to universities and colleges?
2. Should black Americans receive preferential treatment in being hired for a job? in being promoted?
3. Are blacks and whites equal?

4. Are blacks treated equally with whites in the United States today?
5. Would you vote for a qualified black if he or she were to run for President?
6. If you have children, do you allow them to play with both black and white children?
7. Would you be concerned if your child brought home a friend of a different race for dinner?
8. Should blacks and whites be allowed to intermarry?
9. Would you be concerned if a relative or close friend married a person of a different race?
10. All in all, do you feel that anti-black feeling is on the rise in America today, is diminishing, or is about the same as it has been?

H. Writing a Summary

One of the important skills for success in an American university is the ability to write a summary. After carefully rereading the section of the chapter entitled "The Assimilation of Non-Protestant and Non-Western Europeans," write a summary of it in your own words. Your summary should be between 100 and 150 words in length.

I. Paraphrasing

In order to increase your command of English and to make sure you understand what you are reading, it is a good idea to paraphrase important passages, that is, to restate in your own words what the writer has said. Reread the section of the chapter entitled "The Establishment of the Dominant Culture" and paraphrase this section.

J. Ask Americans

Ask at least five Americans to tell you about their ethnic backgrounds.

1. What nationalities were their ancestors?
2. When did their ancestors immigrate to America?
3. Does anyone in their family still speak the language of the "old" (original) country?
4. Do they maintain contact with any relatives in the old country?
5. What family customs or traditions from the old country are there?

K. What's Your Opinion?

A fundamental belief of Americans, which has always attracted immigrants to the United States, is stated in the opening lines of the Declaration of Independence:

> We hold these truths to be self-evident: that all men are created equal, that they are endowed by their Creator with certain inalienable rights; that among these are life, liberty, and the pursuit of happiness.

Do you agree with these "self-evident truths"? Are all people created equal? Do people have a right to life, liberty, and the pursuit of happiness? What ways have other countries tried to ensure similar goals?

L. Suggestions for Research

1. Get a copy of the latest U.S. census data in a recent almanac and find out how closely blacks come to whites in:
   a. Annual income of two-parent families
   b. Annual income of one-parent families
   c. Home ownership
   d. High school graduation
   e. College attendance/graduation
2. Find out how many black men and women are holding political office in the United States. Notice especially how many mayors of southern towns or cities are black.
3. In recent years the United States has begun to question its open door policy on immigration and acceptance of refugees. Look for articles in magazines and newspapers on this subject. What is the general opinion expressed in most of these articles?

M. Suggestions for Writing

Look for information on Martin Luther King, Jr. and choose one of the following composition topics.

1. A brief (two page) summary of his life
2. A report on his use of non-violent demonstrations to bring about social change
3. A summary of his famous "I have a dream" speech

Puerto Rican Day Parade. *Marc Anderson.*

N. Suggestions for Further Reading

Harriet Beecher Stowe. *Uncle Tom's Cabin.*
Claude Brown. *Manchild in the Promised Land.*
Eldridge Cleaver. *Soul on Ice.*
William Faulkner. *Light in August.*
Michael Novak. *The Rise of the Unmeltable Ethnics: Politics and Culture in the Seventies.*
Arthur P. Davis and Saunders Redding, Eds. *Cavalcade: Negro American Writing from 1760 to the Present.*

Graduation day at Fairleigh Dickinson University. *Ken Karp.*

chapter 9

Education in the United States

Americans regard education as the means by which the inequalities among individuals are to be erased and by which every desirable end is to be achieved.

George S. Counts

A student was telling her American friends how difficult it is to get into a university back in her country. "There are not enough universities," she explained, "so there is not room for all the high school students who want to go to a university. Students must pass a very difficult exam to be admitted, and only a few can make it. There is so much competition that students start to prepare very early. Some parents send their children to a good elementary school so they can get into a good high school and then a good university. It is very hard. All through school, my mother told me to study, study every night." "It's not that difficult to get into a college in the United States," said the American. "Of course, some universities are more competitive than others, but there are so many schools that just about everybody has an opportunity to go to college. A lot of students fail or drop out, but they have still had their chance. Americans believe everybody should have the opportunity to go to college."

The Establishment of Public Schools in America: Tocqueville's Observations

As might be expected, educational institutions in the United States reflect the nation's basic values, especially the ideal of equality of opportunity. From elementary school through college, Americans believe that everyone deserves an equal opportunity to get a good education.

From the beginning, when Americans established their basic system of public schools in 1825, they **reaffirmed** the principle of equality by making schools open to all classes of Americans and financing these by taxes collected from all citizens. Those who favored these public schools believed that these institutions would help reduce social class distinctions in the United States by educating children of all social classes in the same "common schools," as they were known at the time. Some wealthier Americans opposed these schools, believing that social class barriers were desirable and that public schools would educate people beyond their "proper station" in life. Such arguments proved weak in a nation where equality of opportunity was such a strong value. By 1860, free public elementary schools (grades 1-8) were firmly established in the United States.

When Alexis de Tocqueville arrived in the United States in 1831, he found a great deal of enthusiasm about the new and growing public elementary schools. The mayor of New York City gave a special dinner for Tocqueville during which a **toast** was offered in honor of "Education—the extension of our public schools—a national blessing."

Because he was a French aristocrat, Tocqueville at first shared the fear of those wealthier Americans who believed that universal education would be a danger rather than a national blessing. He eventually decided , however, that the tendency of public education to encourage people to seek a higher status in life was in harmony with, not in conflict with, the customs of American society. The ideal of equal opportunity for all regardless of family background was much stronger in the United States than in France.

Tocqueville also noted that American public education had a strong practical content which included the teaching of vocational skills and the duties of citizenship. Thus, public education not only gave Americans the desire to better themselves, but it also gave them the practical tools to do so. Moreover, the material abundance of the United States provided material rewards for those who took full advantage of the opportunity for a public education.

During the next century and a half, public schools in the United States were expanded to include secondary or high schools (grades 9-12) and colleges and universities with both undergraduate and graduate studies.

The Educational Ladder

Americans view their public school system as an educational ladder, rising from elementary school to high school and finally college undergraduate and graduate programs. Undergraduate studies lead to a bachelor's degree, which is generally what Americans mean when they speak of a "college **diploma**." The bachelor's degree can be followed by professional studies, which lead to degrees in such professions as law and medicine, and graduate studies, which lead to master's and doctoral degrees.

The educational ladder concept is an almost perfect reflection of the American ideal of individual success based on equality of opportunity and on "working your way to the top."

In the United States there are no separate educational systems with higher education for the wealthy and a lower level of education for the masses. Rather, there is one system which is open to all. Individuals may climb as high on the ladder as they can. The abilities of the individuals, rather than their social class background, are expected to determine how high each person will get.

The educational ladder provided by the public schools does not, however, achieve complete equality of opportunity. There have always been private schools at all levels which are not supported primarily by public funds. Some of these are open to all social classes and some are not. There are a number of private religious schools, for example, which are associated with particular churches and receive financial support from them. Their primary purpose is usually to give religious instruction to children. Their intent is not to maintain social class distinctions, and most of their students are middle class. The most numerous of these, the Catholic

City schoolchildren playing in a schoolyard. *HUD, David Valdez.*

schools, have students whose social class backgrounds are similar to the majority of students in public schools.

There are, however, other private schools that are not open to everyone. These are **elite** private schools which serve mainly upper-class children. Students must pay high **tuition** costs that only wealthier families can afford. Parents often send their children to these schools so that they will associate with other upper-class children and maintain the upper-class position held by their parents.

Unlike private religious schools, elitist private schools do conflict with the American ideal of equality of opportunity represented by the public schools. Private schools often give an extra educational and social advantage to those young people who have the money to attend them. However, because they are relatively few in number, they do not displace the public school as the central educational institution in the United States. Nor does the best private school education protect young people from competition with public school graduates for the best jobs the nation has to offer.

Imperfections in the educational ladder concept can also be seen at its higher levels in university programs. All university students must pay tuition expenses. These are much lower at public universities than at private ones, and thus wealthy students are better able to attend the more expensive, and sometimes better, private universities. Even at public universities the expenses of buying books and living away from home make it difficult for poor students to attend.

Despite its imperfections, Americans continue to believe in public education as the ladder to success in life. Their belief has been confirmed by experience. In 1900, for example, less than 10 percent of young Americans entered college. Today over 30 percent of the total population of Americans over 21 have attended college. There are about 10 million students attending college now, about seven times more than forty years ago, and there are some 3,000 different colleges and universities to choose from. The rapid growth of public universities supported by government funds has made this expansion possible. Today many parents who were not able to attend college when they were young have the satisfaction of seeing their sons and daughters attend.

EDUCATION: ONE-HALF ARE UPWARDLY MOBILE

Question: What is the highest grade in elementary school or high school that (you/your father) finished and got credit for? (If finished 9th-12th grade or don't know) Did (you/he) ever get a high school diploma or a GED certificate? Did (you/he) complete one or more years of college for credit—not including schooling such as business college, technical or vocational school. Do you (Does he) have any college degrees?

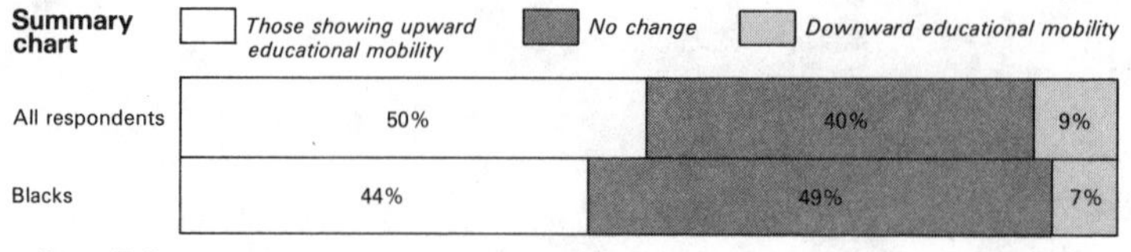

Public Opinion, June/July 1982

Even the formerly elitist private universities have yielded a great deal to public pressure for greater equality of opportunity in education. Harvard, a private university considered by many to be the nation's most prestigious, provides a good example. "There has been a startling change in who gets into Harvard over the past 25 years—startling," reports the director of admissions at Harvard. Before World War II, he says, about two-thirds of the students admitted to the university came from elite private preparatory schools. By contrast, more than three-quarters of those accepted in 1980 were public school graduates.

As equality of opportunity came to Harvard, the competition that accompanies it also increased dramatically. Before World War II Harvard admitted about 90 percent of those who applied. These applicants were mostly wealthy private school graduates who, in the words of one journalist, "knew their place and their place was Harvard." By 1980 thousands of bright middle-class students in public schools had come to believe that Harvard just might be their place. The university received 14,000 applications for admission in that year and accepted 2,148, only about 15 percent of the applicants.

The Money Value of Education

As we have seen in earlier chapters, the American definition of success is largely one of acquiring wealth and a high material standard of living. It is not surprising, therefore, that Americans have valued education for its **monetary** value. The belief is widespread in the United States that the more schooling people have, the more money they will earn when they leave school. The belief is strongest regarding the desirability of an undergraduate university degree, or a professional degree such as medicine or law following the undergraduate degree. The money value of graduate degrees in "nonprofessional" fields such as art, history, or philosophy is not as great.

This belief in the monetary value of education is supported by statistics on income. Ben Wattenberg, a social scientist, estimated that in the course of a lifetime a man with a college degree in 1972 would earn about $380,000 more than a man with just a high school diploma. Perhaps this helps to explain survey findings which showed that Americans who wished they had lived their lives differently in some way regretted most of all that they did not get more education.

The regret is shared by those who have made it to the top and by those who have not. Journalist Richard Reeves quotes a black worker in a Ford automobile factory:

> When I was in the ninth grade, I was getting bad grades and messing around. My father came home in the kitchen one night with a pair of Ford work pants and he threw them in my face. "Put these on," he said, "because you're going to be wearing them the rest of your life if you don't get an education."

Douglas Fraser, the president of the United Auto Workers Union, regretted not finishing high school so much that he occasionally lied about it. He told Richard Reeves about his pride in graduating from high school, but then a few minutes later he said:

> I wasn't telling the truth about high school. I never finished. I quit in the twelfth grade to take a job .... It's funny—after all these years, I still lie about it. Because the fact is, I still think it was a stupid thing to do. I should have finished my education.

Even a man like Fraser, a nationally known and successful leader, was troubled by regrets that he did not climb higher on the educational ladder.

Ken Karp.

Extracurricular Activities

While it is true that Americans believe climbing the educational ladder leads to success, they are less certain that intellectual achievement, which is the main purpose of the schools, is the only important factor leading to success. A competitive—even aggressive—personality is seen as important to success, especially in men. The development of social and political skills are also considered to be very important.

To help Americans develop these other important skills, schools have added a large number of **extracurricular** activities (activities outside classroom studies) to daily life at school. This is especially true of high schools and colleges but extends down into elementary schools as well.

Athletics, frequently called "competitive sports," are perhaps the most important of these activities. Football, basketball, and baseball teams are seen as very important in teaching students, particularly boys, the "winning spirit." At times, athletic teams seem to become more important to some students and their parents than the academic programs offered by the schools.

Student government is another extracurricular activity designed to develop competitive, political, and social skills in students. The students choose a number of student government officers, who compete for the votes of their fellow students in schoolwide elections. Although these officers have little power over the central decisions of the school, the process of running for office and then taking responsibility for a number of minor matters if elected is seen as good experience in developing their leadership and competitive skills.

Athletics and student government are only two of a variety of extracurricular activities found in American schools. There are clubs and activities for almost every student interest, all aimed at helping the student to become more successful in later life. Many parents watch their children's extracurricular activities with as much interest and concern as they do their children's intellectual achievements in the classroom.

Racial Equality and Education

The most significant departure from the ideal of equality of opportunity in education occurred in the education of black Americans. As we saw in the previous chapter, after the Civil War in the 1860s the southern states developed a social system which segregated the former black slaves from the white population in all public facilities, including schools. Black people in the southern states were **prohibited** by law from attending schools with whites. Blacks had separate schools which were inferior to the white schools by almost any measure.

In 1896 the Supreme Court of the United States stated that racial segregation in public schools and other public facilities in the southern states did not **violate** the Constitution. Equality of opportunity was such an important American value that the Supreme Court had to pretend that the separate black schools and other facilities were equal to those of whites, when everyone knew that they were not. The Supreme Court invented what is called the "separate but equal doctrine" to justify racial segregation in public schools and other public facilities in the southern states.

Justice John Marshall Harlan strongly disagreed with the decision of his fellow justices. The decision, he said, did a great injustice to black people in the United States. Moreover, it violated the nation's highest law and its basic values. "Our Constitution is color-blind," he said, "and neither knows nor tolerates classes among its citizens."

Fifty-eight years later a more modern Supreme Court agreed with Justice Harlan. In a historic decision in 1954 it held that laws that forced black students to go to racially segregated schools violated the U.S. Constitution because such schools could never be equal. The opinion of the Court was that "to separate [black schoolchildren] from others ... solely because of their race generates a feeling of inferiority ... that may affect their hearts and minds in a way unlikely ever to be undone."

The Supreme Court's decision in 1954 led to changes which brought an end to the system of segregated public education in the southern states. However, problems in race relations continued to trouble the public schools, even though schools were legally desegregated throughout the country.

Black Americans were still mainly in the lowest income and occupational groups and frequently lived in **slums** in the nation's largest cities. The public schools in these areas were composed predominantly or entirely of black students and often shared the neighborhood problems of high crime rates and other forms of social disorder. The schools in the black slums were clearly unequal to those in the predominantly white, middle-class neighborhoods.

The problem of schools where racial separation results from the makeup of neighborhoods rather than from laws requiring segregation exists in all parts of the United States, not just in the South. Numerous efforts to solve this problem have not succeeded very well. The most **controversial** method used to deal with unequal neighborhood schools was the busing of schoolchildren from their home neighborhoods to schools in more distant neighborhoods in order to achieve a greater mixture of black and white children in all schools. Black children from poor or slum neighborhoods were bused to schools in predominantly white middle-class neighborhoods, and students living in the middle-class neighborhoods were bused into the poorer black neighborhood schools.

The debate over school busing continues with no clear agreement among Americans as to whether or not it has succeeded in increasing equal opportunity in the field of public education. Polls indicate that the overwhelming majority of whites oppose busing to achieve racial balance in public schools, and many blacks also oppose it. It is doubtful that the white majority would have tolerated the amount of busing that has taken place if the ideal of equality of opportunity were not so strong in the American culture.

A new question dealing with racial equality in education was brought to the Supreme Court in the late 1970s. The question dealt with the admissions policies of professional schools, such as medical and law schools, which are attached to many of the nation's colleges and universities. Some of these schools have attempted to do more than treat all applicants equally. Many have tried in recent years to make up for past discrimination against blacks and other minorities by setting aside a certain number of places specifically for applicants from these groups. This practice came to be described as setting minority **quotas**, lowering somewhat the academic standards for admission for a limited number of minority applicants.

A 1975 anti-busing demonstration in Washington, D.C. *UPI.*

This could be seen as special treatment rather than equal opportunity. However, many professional school administrators believed that because of discrimination against these groups in the past, equality now demanded that certain limited numbers of minority students be given some extra advantage in the selection of new professional students.

These quotas were challenged by a white student, Allen Bakke, who was denied admission to the medical school at the University of California at Davis, California. He claimed that the medical school had admitted some nonwhite minority students less qualified than he. The U.S. Supreme Court in the famous *Bakke Case* of 1978 agreed that he had been denied an equal opportunity for admission. In a rather complicated decision, the Court held that a professional school could not set aside a certain number of places to be filled only by minority students. Such quotas were a denial of equal educational opportunity. Professional schools, however, could give some extra consideration to nonwhite minority applicants, but the Court was forbidding them to carry this practice too far.

The Increasing Responsibilities of Public Schools

In 1982 the Supreme Court took the bold step of saying that an entirely new group of students must be given an equal opportunity to receive a public education. The new students were the children of **aliens** who are living in the

United States illegally. The state of Texas required that this group of students, unlike other students, pay tuition to enter its public elementary schools. The Supreme Court said that the state of Texas could not do this. The state must treat the children of illegal aliens on the same basis as it treated other students.

Americans place the weight of many of their ideals, hopes, and problems on the nation's public school system. Some observers believe they have placed more responsibilities on the public schools than the schools can possibly handle. For example, as noted above, school busing plans have been required of the public schools in an attempt to solve the problems that result from certain neighborhoods being predominantly poor and predominantly black.

While the benefits of the busing plans are debatable, they have clearly put a strain on public education and have contributed to an overall decline in citizen support for the public schools.

In addition to dealing with these problems, the public schools are usually expected to solve student problems that result from the weakening of family ties in the United States. For example, rising divorce rates have resulted in an increasing number of children in the public schools who are raised by only one parent. Studies have shown that these children are more likely to get into trouble at school than are children raised in families with two parents. The public schools are forced to deal with a larger number of children from weakened families who may not have been taught proper behavior at home.

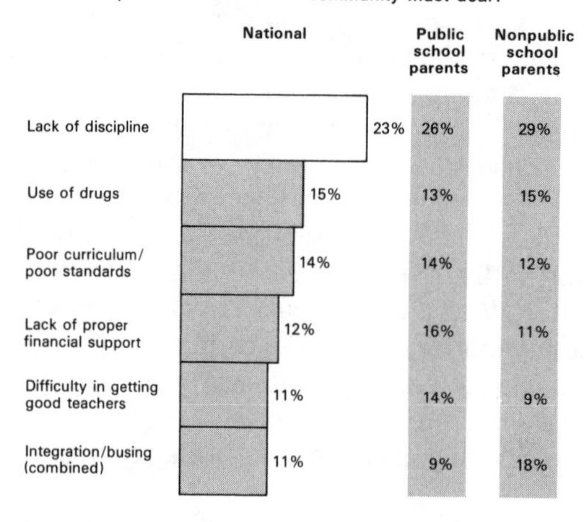

Public Opinion, October/November 1981

At a time when enormous new **burdens** are being placed on the public schools, the nation finds itself faced with new limits on its material abundance. These limits have steadily reduced the amount of money available to the public schools as they try to deal with their rapidly growing problems.

Throughout the nation's history, most Americans have seen the public school system as a great educational ladder of opportunity. Beginning in the late 1960s, however, many Americans came to see more problems than opportunities when they observed the public schools in action. This has resulted in a serious decline in citizen support for the public schools.

Americans have expected much and received much from their public schools since they began in the early 1800s. No institution has done more to develop equality of opportunity in the nation. Recent decades, however, point to the danger that if Americans expect too much from their public schools, they may receive too little.

In spite of these dangers, public education is likely to remain one of the most important institutions in American society. Although it has many flaws, no acceptable substitute for it has yet been found.

Children's Bureau, Department of Health and Human Services. Dick Swartz.

New Words

reaffirm affirm again; to state or declare again
toast a call on people to drink to the honor of someone or something; the words spoken before drinking
diploma an official paper showing that a person has successfully finished a course of study or passed an examination
elite serving the best or most important people in a social group
tuition the money paid for instruction at a college or private school
monetary having to do with money
extracurricular refers to activities outside regular academic class work
prohibit to forbid by law; to prevent
violate to act against; to be against a law or rule
slum an area in a city with poor living conditions and dirty, unrepaired buildings
controversial causing much argument or disagreement
quota a stated number or amount; a limit on numbers
alien a foreigner who has not become a citizen of the country where he or she is living
burden a heavy load or responsibility; a duty that is hard to accomplish

A. Vocabulary Check

Fill in the blank with the correct word from the new word list.

1. In 1954 the Supreme Court ruled that segregation denied black children an equal opportunity to an education and it therefore ______ the Constitution.
2. Private schools that admit only the richest and most important people in society are ______.
3. School activities outside regular academic class work are ______.
4. A duty that is difficult to perform is a ______.
5. An official paper showing that a person has successfully finished a course of study is called a ______.
6. An area in a city with poor living conditions and dirty, unrepaired buildings is a ______.
7. The money students pay for instruction at a private school or college is called ______.
8. An idea that causes much argument or disagreement is ______.
9. A problem involving money is a ______ problem.
10. If you state again something that you believe, you are ______ your belief.
11. A foreigner who has not become a citizen of the country where he or she is living is an ______.

12. Something that is forbidden by law is ______.
13. In order to ensure that a certain number of minority people will be admitted to a professional school, the school may set ______.
14. Before drinking an alcoholic beverage, it is customary to offer a ______ and ask people to drink in honor of someone or something.

B. Comprehension Check

Write the letter of the best answer according to the information in the chapter.

____ 1. Some wealthier Americans opposed the first public schools in the United States because
- a. they cost too much money.
- b. they would weaken social class barriers.
- c. they went against the idea of competition.

____ 2. Tocqueville finally concluded that universal public education in America would
- a. give Americans not only the desire but also the means to better their position in life.
- b. not provide any practical training in vocational skills.
- c. not work because people would have the desire to rise to a higher social class but they would be prevented from doing so by the aristocracy.

____ 3. The *main* ideal on which the educational ladder is based in the United States is
- a. hard work.
- b. self-reliance.
- c. equality of opportunity.

____ 4. Between 1900 and the 1980s the percentage of young Americans who attended college
- a. increased enormously.
- b. stayed about the same.
- c. decreased slightly.

____ 5. What most Americans like most about higher education is
- a. its cultural value.
- b. its monetary value.
- c. its moral value.

____ 6. Which of the following would *not* be considered an extracurricular activity?
- a. a school baseball team
- b. the student government of a school
- c. a classroom research project

____ 7. Private religious schools are viewed by most Americans as
   a. being opposed to the ideal of equality of opportunity.
   b. not being opposed to the ideal of equality of opportunity.
   c. being elitist in their purpose.

____ 8. In 1896 the U.S. Supreme Court said that racially segregated public facilities
   a. violated the principle of equality.
   b. violated the U.S. Constitution.
   c. did not violate the principle of equality or the U.S. Constitution.

____ 9. Public schools that are mainly black or mainly white today usually are the result of
   a. the racial makeup of neighborhoods.
   b. laws that separate racial groups.
   c. Supreme Court decisions that separate racial groups.

____ 10. In the case involving Allen Bakke, a professional school
   a. refused to admit him as a student because he belonged to a minority group.
   b. admitted students less qualified than Bakke because they were members of minority groups.
   c. refused to admit him as a student because he had said unfavorable things about the school.

C. Questions for Discussion and Composition

1. Is education compulsory in your country? If so, how long is a child required by law to stay in school? Are there both public and private schools in your country? What are these schools like? What kind of school did you attend?
2. Are there enough universities in your country to serve most young people? Is it necessary to take a national examination to get into a university? Is there a lot of competition?
3. Are most schools in your country coeducational? Do women receive a different education than men do? Are all fields of education open to women?
4. Do many people raise their social class level by getting an education in your country? How rich do you have to be to attend a university in your country? How much tuition do you have to pay? Are there many scholarships available?
5. How interested is your government in universal education? How much intellectual freedom does the government permit in your schools? Does your government determine the course of study at all high schools? Does your government have a scholarship program to encourage students to study abroad?
6. Are there extracurricular activities in high schools and colleges in your country? If so, what are they? Are they important? Did you participate in nonacademic clubs or activities in high school in your country?

7. What is the role of the teacher in your country? Is it possible for teachers and students to be friends? Would a student ever be invited to a professor's home in your country? How strict is discipline in the schools?

D. Cloze Summary Paragraph

This paragraph summarizes the chapter. Fill in each blank with any word that makes sense.

From the time when ___*the*___ system of public education ________ established in America in ________ the ideal of equality ________ opportunity has been reaffirmed ________ education. Although Tocqueville and ________ of the wealthier Americans ________ about the consequences of ________ education, the system has ________ people both the desire ________ raise their standard of ________ and the means to ________ so. Americans think of ________ system as an educational ________ which should give people ________ equal opportunity to climb ________ high as they wish. ________ children attend private religious ________ and there are some ________ private schools for upper-________ children, but most Americans ________ public school. About one-third ________ all adults have attended ________ and most people believe ________ graduating from college results ________ a higher paying job. ________ Americans regret not getting ________ education. In addition to ________ work, schools provide extracurricular ________ which develop competitive, social, ______________ political skills. Public schools ______________ tried to correct inequalities ______________ by racial segregation through ______________ and minority quotas. Today ______________ must deal with children ______________ broken homes and ______________ social problems while facing ______________ loss of money and ______________ support.

E. Outlining

In this exercise you will complete an outline for the chapter. The entries to go in the blanks are listed at the end of the outline. They are scrambled, so you must check the order of the information by skimming the chapter. Be sure to choose the most general headings for the Roman numeral entries.

Introduction: The ideal of equality of opportunity in American education

I. The establishment of public schools in America
   A. Characteristics of public schools
   B. Reasons why the wealthy feared universal education
   C. Tocqueville's observations

II. The educational ladder
   A. ______________________________
   B. Types of private schools
   C. Why the number attending college has increased

III. ______________________________
   A. ______________________________
   B. Regrets of those who did not get enough education

IV. ______________________________
   A. ______________________________
   B. ______________________________

V. ______________________________

A. ______________________________
B. Efforts to improve black education after segregation ended
C. ______________________________

VI. ______________________________

A. ______________________________
B. The burden of busing
C. ______________________________

Scrambled Entries

The increasing responsibilities of public schools
The use of quotas to give blacks a chance to catch up
Why extracurricular activities are seen as important
The segregation of blacks from whites in schools
The belief that a college education brings jobs with higher pay
Racial equality and education
Description of ladder
Education of the children of aliens
Extracurricular activities
Types of extracurricular activities
The money value of education
Other problems facing schools

F. Ask Americans

Find out how Americans feel about education. Ask Americans the following questions and record the answers.

1. Should there be prayer in the public school?
2. Are you for or against busing to achieve racial balance in the schools?
3. Should poor children be given free lunches at school?
4. Should there be sex education in the schools? If so, should it be taught in elementary school, high school, or both?
5. How much exposure to drugs is there at the schools in your neighborhood? Is this a problem?
6. How important is a college education? Will it give you more status? Will you make more money with a college education?
7. Is it important which college you attend, or are all colleges about the same?

8. What is the highest level of education your parents had? (What was the last grade completed or degree received?)
9. What is the highest level of education you have received? Do you expect to get any more education?

G. Ask Yourself

What should be taught in public high schools? What should be the priorities? Read the following list of areas which are covered in American schools and decide which are the most important. Arrange the items in order from most important to least important.

1. Developing students' moral and ethical character
2. Teaching students how to think
3. Preparing students who do not go to college for a job or career after graduation
4. Preparing students to become informed citizens prepared to vote at 18
5. Preparing students for college
6. Developing students' appreciation of art, music, and other cultural pursuits
7. Other (your opinion)

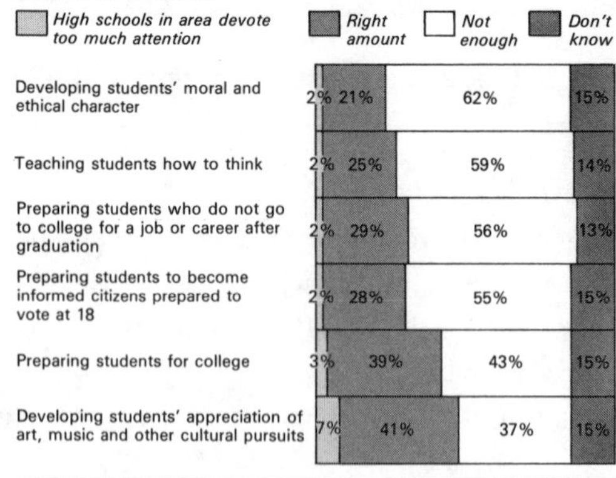

Public Opinion, October/November 1981

H. Skimming

Skim the chapter to find the following information.

1. When public schools were first established in the United States
2. What the mayor of New York City said in his toast at the dinner for Tocqueville
3. What percentage of young people went to college in 1900
4. What startling change has occurred at Harvard in the last 25 years
5. What the Supreme Court ruled in 1954 about segregated schools
6. Who Allen Bakke was

I. People Watching

1. When is the "right" time to ask a question in an American classroom? Watch others and notice the following. (If you have difficulty finding the answers to these questions, ask a fellow student or ask the teacher to explain when is the right time for questions.)
   a. Is the teacher talking when students ask questions?
   b. How do students indicate that they have a question to ask?
   c. How does the teacher indicate that he or she is ready for questions? Does the teacher ask, "Are there any questions?"
   Does the teacher pause and look up from notes or from the blackboard?
   d. What other signals does a teacher send to indicate that questions are invited?
2. One of the most difficult things for students to understand is when an interview or an appointment with a teacher or professor is over. How do you know when the interview has ended? Watch a teacher and student in an interview or appointment, if possible, and see which of these are used to indicate the appointment is over. If you cannot observe a teacher and student, perhaps you can watch at another similar situation such as a job interview, a meeting with a counselor, or an appointment with a doctor. Look for the following.
   a. The teacher moves noticeably in the chair—maybe closer to the desk or toward the door.
   b. The teacher says, "Well . . ." or "It has been nice talking to you" or "I think you understand now . . . ."
   c. The teacher turns his or her attention to other business such as papers on the desk or a schedule of appointments.
   d. The teacher moves the chair back from the desk.

J. Compare and Contrast

Schools around the world differ in their expectations of students. In some schools students are expected only to listen and remember what their teachers say; in others they are expected to ask questions. It's important to know these differences if you are going to be successful in a school in another country.

First answer the following questions, using True or False, to indicate how you think students should behave in your country. Record those answers in one column. Then ask an American (preferably a student) for his or her opinion and record those answers in a second column. What differences do you notice? Compare your answers with those of your classmates.

1. Students should not ask questions; they should only answer them.
2. Students should rise when the teacher enters the classroom.
3. A teacher should be challenged or disagreed with in class.
4. Students should never address teachers by their first names.
5. Students should memorize everything their teachers say; education is primarily memorizing books and teachers' lectures.
6. Male and female students should attend the same classes.

University of Utah.

K. Suggestions for Writing

1. Why do Americans respect people who have worked their way through college, that is, who have paid for their own college education by working while they were also attending classes? What values does this reveal? Write a paragraph of explanation.
2. What do you think the real value of education is? Is it monetary? Is it intellectual stimulation?
3. Who should attend college? Should everyone? Why or why not? Is anyone too old to attend college? Too young?
4. Studies show that 50 percent of Americans have more education than their fathers did and that education is the single most important factor in upward mobility—more important than ethnic background. Discuss what upward mobility means to Americans and how that reflects the basic American values of self-reliance, progress, and bettering oneself.

L. Suggestions for Further Reading

Ralph Waldo Emerson. *The American Scholar.*
Leonard Q. Ross. *The Education of Hyman Kaplan.*
Charles Silberman. *Crisis in the Classroom.*

Western Kentucky University. Gary Hairlson.

chapter 10

Organized Sports and Recreation

The form and type of play and sports life which evolve in any group or nation mirror the development in other segments of the culture.

American Academy of Physical Education

A student in an American university was telling one of his teachers about the kinds of things he tells new students who arrive in the United States from his country. "There are many things I have to tell them," he said. "I have to explain to them about girls wearing shorts. They will be very confused because in my country, if a girl goes out on the street wearing shorts, she can be arrested by the police." The American teacher laughed. "I can imagine that it would be quite a shock for them," she said, "when they see women in shorts out jogging." The student agreed. "Jogging is popular back home, but not for women. In the United States, everybody jogs—young people, old people—everybody. I can look out of my dorm window any time of day or night and see somebody out jogging."

Sports and American Values

Most social scientists believe that sports that are organized by a society generally reflect the basic values of that society and attempt to strengthen them in the minds and emotions of its people. Therefore, organized sports have a more serious social purpose than spontaneous, unorganized play by individuals. This is certainly true in the United States, where the three major organized sports are football, basketball, and baseball. Nowhere are the ways and words of democracy better illustrated than in sports.

Organized sports are seen by Americans as an inspiring example of equality of opportunity in action. In sports, people of different races and economic backgrounds get an equal chance to excel. For this reason, notes sociologist Harry Edwards, Americans view organized sports "as a laboratory in which young men, regardless of social class, can learn the advantages and rewards of a competitive system."

The idea of competition is at the very heart of organized sports in the United States. Learning how to win in sports is believed to develop the habits necessary to compete successfully in later life. This training, in turn, strengthens American society as a whole. "It is commonly held," says one sports writer, "that the competitive ethic taught in sports must be learned and **ingrained** in youth for the future success of American business and military efforts."

The competitive ethic in organized sports contains some elements of hard work—often called "**hustle**," **persistence**, or "never quitting"—and of physical courage—being "tough" or having "**guts**." Slogans are sometimes used to drive home the competitive virtues for the young participants: "Hustle—you can't survive without it." "A quitter never wins; a winner never quits." "It's easy to be ordinary, but it takes guts to excel."

Whereas amateur athletics, associated with the schools and colleges, are valued for teaching young people basic American values, professional sports, in addition to their profit and entertainment purposes, are seen as providing an example to inspire the young to take part in organized sports. In the process of serving as an inspiration for basic American values, organized sports have become part of what was referred to in Chapter 3 as "the national religion," a mixture of patriotism and national pride on the one hand with religious ideas and symbols on the other.

The bringing together of sports, religion, and national values can be illustrated by the 1971 Rose Bowl game. The Rose Bowl is the most prestigious of several special football games played every New Year's Day among the nation's best college football teams. Billy Graham, a famous American Protestant religious leader, was made the leading figure in the 1971 Rose Bowl parade. In that role he spoke out in favor of the moral value of sports in American society: "The Bible says leisure and lying around are morally dangerous . . . sports keep us busy . . . . There are probably more really committed Christians in sports, both collegiate and professional, than in any other occupation in America."

Criticism of American Values

Although sports in the United States are glorified by many, there are others who are especially critical of the power of sports to corrupt when certain things are carried to excess. An excessive desire to win in sports, for example, can corrupt rather than strengthen American values.

Critics have pointed out that too many coaches and players have done just this. Vince Lombardi, a famous professional football coach of the 1960s, was often criticized for stating that winning is the "only thing" that matters in sports. Critics believe that such statements by coaches weaken the idea that other things, such as fair play, following the rules of the game, and behaving with dignity when one is defeated, are also important. Unfortunately, many coaches share Lombardi's "winning is the only thing" philosophy. Woody Hayes, another of the most famous football coaches in the United States, once said: "Anyone who tells me, 'Don't worry that you lost; you played a good game anyway,' I just hate."

Despite the view expressed by such coaches as Lombardi and Hayes, there is a tradition of honorable defeat in American sports. Sociologist Harry Edwards, for example, has pointed out that "The all-important significance of winning is known, but likewise, there is the **consoling** 'reward' of the 'honorable defeat.' Indeed, the 'sweetness' of winning is derived . . . from the knowledge of having defeated a courageous opponent who performed honorably."

When the idea of winning in sports is carried to excess, honorable competition can turn into disorder and violence. In one game the players of two professional baseball teams became so angry at each other that the game turned into a large-scale fight between the two teams. The coach of one of the teams was happy about the fight because, in the games that followed, his team consistently won. He thought that the fight had helped to bring the men on his team closer together. Similarly, a professional football coach stated: "If we didn't go out there

Western Kentucky University. Mike Douglas.

and fight, I'd be worried. You go out there and protect your teammates. The guys who sit on the bench, they're the losers." Both coaches seemed to share the view that if occasional fights with opposing teams helped to increase the winning spirit of their players, so much the better.

Violence in American sports has been increasingly criticized in recent years by those who approve of sports generally and who believe that violence is corrupting it. Most of the criticism has been directed toward football, perhaps America's favorite popular sport. Such respected publications as *Reader's Digest*, the most widely read popular magazine in the United States, and *Sports Illustrated*, the nation's leading sports magazine, have both criticized the number of injuries that have resulted from the extreme roughness of the game, increased by a burning desire to defeat one's opponent.

A few critics believe that sports should be completely replaced by noncompetitive kinds of **recreation**. These critics tend to be strongly opposed to the basic American value of competition as well. They view the emphasis on competition in American life as having corrupted the entire culture. As a first step in eliminating this corruption, they want to abolish organized sports.

Americans generally are not sympathetic to this harsh criticism of organized sports. Competition, they believe, strengthens the national character rather than corrupting it. They believe that eliminating competition in sports and in society as a whole would lead to laziness and vice rather than hard work and accomplishment. One high school principal, for example, described the harsh criticism of competitive sports as "the revolutionaries' attempt to break down the basic foundations upon which the society is founded." Comments of this sort illustrate how strong the idea of competition is in the United States and how important organized sports are as a means of maintaining this value in the larger society.

Male and Female Roles

The strong tie between organized sports and the competitive ethic has given greater importance to men's sports than to women's, since man's role in the United States is viewed as more competitive and aggressive than woman's. As one high school teacher stated more than two decades ago: "Our culture does not require girls to compete against each other in physical activity to achieve the acceptable female image. Our culture does require boys to do so."

During the last fifteen years, however, this has been changing, and a stronger emphasis on equality for women has emerged in all facets of American life, including organized sports. High schools and colleges have been urged to give more emphasis to women's sports and to spend more money on them. In fact, laws governing equality have required many schools to do so.

It is still true, however, that most Americans believe men's organized sports are more important than women's. In high school, and to a lesser extent in college, males earn popularity and recognition through competing in organized sports, while females often earn these same things by being cheerleaders. The

A college cheerleader at a basketball game.
Western Kentucky University. Gary Hairlson.

cheerleader does not compete. Rather, she is part of a group of pretty girls who lead the people watching football or basketball games in cheering for the school team, which is composed of competitive young men.

The difference in roles between the males and females at major sports events reflects differences in traditional roles later in life, when men are expected to compete for economic success and the women are supposed to give men emotional support as wives and homemakers. Although these roles also are changing in American society (see the next chapter), the basic expectation that men should be more competitive than women still **endures**. Organized sports both reflect and strengthen this expectation.

Recreation: A Time for Self-Improvement

Unlike organized sports, what is generally called recreation in the United States is not expected to encourage competition. For this reason, it is much more spontaneous and serves the individual's needs beyond the competitive world of work. Nevertheless, much can be learned about the values of Americans from an examination of the kinds of recreation in which they engage.

Many Americans prefer recreation that requires a high level of physical activity. This is true of the three fastest growing adult recreational sports: jogging or running, tennis, and snow skiing. It would seem that Americans carry over their belief in hard work into their world of play and recreation. The well-known expression "we like to work hard and play hard" is an example of this philosophy.

Over the last fifteen years, for example, jogging has become a popular pastime for 30 million participants of all ages. Joggers seem to **thrive** on the physical activity as they try to run longer and longer distances in shorter and shorter time periods. In 1976 a 57-year-old man gained national recognition by running 164 miles in less than 38 hours in a long-distance race called a marathon. In October 1981, 16,000 runners competed in the 26-mile New York City Marathon. Sports writers noted that only a few of the runners had any hope of winning the marathon. For the vast majority of them, the challenge was to have the physical endurance to finish the 26-mile race.

The high level of physical activity enjoyed by many Americans at play has led to the observation that Americans have difficulty **relaxing**, even in their leisure time. Yet the people who enjoy these physical activities often say that they find

The 26-mile New York Marathon. *Laimute E. Druskis.*

them very relaxing mentally because the activity is so different from the kind of activity they must do in the world of work, often indoor office work involving mind rather than body.

The interest that Americans have in self-improvement, traceable in large measure to the nation's Protestant heritage (see Chapter 3), is also carried over into their recreation habits. It is evident in the jogger who is determined to improve the distance he can run and the time in which he can run it. The self-improvement motive, however, can also be seen in many other popular forms of recreation which involve little or no physical activity.

Interest and participation in cultural activities, which improve one's mind or one's skills, have been growing rapidly in recent years. According to a report in *U.S. News and World Report* magazine, in one year 78 million Americans visited museums, 62 million attended at least one live theater performance, and 78 million participated in some form of artistic activity: painting, performing music, **handicrafts**, and the like. Interest in handicrafts seems to be thriving in the United States. About 40 percent of all Americans are engaged in handicrafts such as candle making, weaving, and wood carving. Handicraft enthusiasts seem to be "imitating through hobbies what they view as ... the more **wholesome** pursuits of **bygone** days."

The recreational interests of Americans also show a continuing respect for the self-reliance, and sometimes the adventure and danger, of frontier life. Handicraft enthusiasts, for example, take pride in being able to begin and finish a complete product, as once was done on the frontier, without dependence on today's big business or big government. In recent years the number of Americans who maintain their own vegetable gardens has also risen. According to one government official in the Department of Agriculture, Americans do not do this primarily to save money; rather, their greatest satisfaction is in growing some of their own food (self-reliance) and in tasting its home-grown flavor.

Some Americans are drawn to hobbies that give them a feeling not only of self-reliance but of adventure and risk as well. An official at Big Bend National Park in Texas reports that about 20,000 people come to the wilderness and mountain areas of the park each year. Many of them like to come in the middle of winter when the hardships are greater. Following the death of two persons in a mountain-climbing accident in the park, campers and climbers came in even greater numbers to the same area where the accidents occurred. "It is as if they are looking for hardship," stated the park official. "They seem to enjoy the danger and the physical challenge."

Americans, like people everywhere, enjoy forms of recreation in which little but rest and relaxation is sought. Watching television, going on picnics, or visiting friends are simply enjoyable ways to pass the time. However, as we have seen, millions of Americans seek new challenges involving new forms of effort even in their leisure time. "Their reward," states *U.S. News and World Report*, "is a renewed sense of **vitality**," a sense of a goal conquered and confidence regained in dealing with life's ups and downs.

New Words

ingrained fixed deep inside so that it is difficult to get out or destroy
hustle aggressive hard work
persistence refusing to stop even if it is difficult to continue
guts courage; determination
consoling giving comfort or sympathy to someone in times of disappointment or sadness
recreation amusement; a way of spending free time
endure to last; to bear pain or suffering
thrive to develop well and be healthy; to grow strong; to be successful
relax to become less active and stop worrying; to unwind; to rest; to become less tight
handicrafts things made by hand
wholesome good for the body; having a good moral effect
bygone gone by; past
vitality life; forcefulness of character or manner; energy and enthusiasm

A. Vocabulary Check

Fill in the crossword puzzle with words from the new word list.

ACROSS

3. good for the body
4. things made by hand
5. refusing to stop
8. amusement; a way to spend time
10. courage; determination
11. life; energy and enthusiasm

DOWN

1. gone by; past
2. giving comfort to someone who is disappointed
6. fixed deep inside
7. aggressive hard work
8. to become less active and stop working
9. to last
12. to develop well and be healthy

B. Comprehension Check

Write the letter of the best answer according to the information in the chapter.

____ 1. Organized sports in a society
   a. are a poor reflection of the values of that society.
   b. are a good reflection of the values of that society.
   c. are leisure activities and games which tell us very little about the social values of a country.

____ 2. Which of the following ideals is *at the very heart* of organized sports in the United States and is therefore the most important ideal expressed in organized sports?
   a. hard work
   b. self-denial
   c. competition

____ 3. Billy Graham's participation in the 1971 Rose Bowl game illustrates
   a. the role sports plays in the national religion.
   b. the enormous popularity of sports among all classes of Americans.
   c. the amount of money spent on sports.

____ 4. Vince Lombardi, a famous professional football coach, expressed the view that
   a. sports help boys grow into men.
   b. a good football player makes a good soldier.
   c. winning is the only thing that matters.

____ 5. Respected publications such as *Reader's Digest* have stated that
   a. sports are good in general, but excessive violence in sports should be stopped.
   b. sports corrupts the American spirit and should be replaced with noncompetitive activities.
   c. many aspects of American culture, such as music and art, have been replaced by the love of sports.

____ 6. American society today generally
  a. gives equal importance to men's sports and to women's sports.
  b. gives greater importance to men's sports than to women's sports.
  c. does not believe that either men's or women's sports serve any useful purpose in maintaining the values of the nation.

____ 7. Cheerleaders at sports events are
  a. usually males.
  b. usually females.
  c. equally divided between males and females.

____ 8. What is generally called "recreation" in the United States
  a. stresses competition less than organized sports.
  b. stresses competition more than organized sports.
  c. stresses competition about the same as organized sports.

____ 9. Some of the fastest growing forms of recreation in the United States, such as jogging, reflect the attitude that
  a. a healthy body helps to maintain a healthy mind.
  b. contact with nature is good for the soul of man.
  c. it is good to work hard and to play hard.

____ 10. Many forms of recreation, such as participation in cultural activities, show an American desire for
  a. self-improvement.
  b. competition.
  c. hard work.

C. Questions for Discussion and Composition

1. What organized sports are popular in your country? Does your country have great pride in its soccer teams? What status do professional athletes have in your country?
2. What sports are played in high schools and colleges in your country? Are college games ever shown on television? How much emphasis on participating in sports is there in your country? Are young people encouraged to play sports? If so, why?
3. Do you agree with Vince Lombardi that "Winning is not the most important thing—it is the *only* thing"? Is competition an important value in your country? Is competition stressed more than cooperation in organized sports? What role do you think sports play in your country?
4. Why do some Americans criticize American football? Is American football played in your country? What do you think of this sport?
5. Why do men and women have different traditional roles in sports in the United States? Is this the situation in your country? Are there cheerleaders in your country?

6. What are popular forms of recreation in your country? Are running and jogging popular? Do many people ski or play tennis? Is there an interest in handicrafts? Do many people have their own gardens? Is camping popular? How much interest in cultural activities is there?
7. What do you like to do in your leisure time? Do you think leisure time is a good opportunity for self-improvement, or is it better to just relax? How would you compare the day-to-day level of activity of people in your country with that of Americans? Do people in your country walk or ride bicycles as often as they drive?

D. Cloze Summary Paragraph

This paragraph is a summary of the chapter. Fill in the blanks with any word that makes sense.

Organized sports in the ___*United*___ States reflect the values ______________ the American people. Americans ______________ in equality of opportunity ______________ sports, but competition is ______________ most important value. They ______________ that participation in sports ______________ healthy and important because ______________ teaches young people how ______________ compete successfully. The emphasis ______________ winning can sometimes lead ______________ violence in sports, and ______________ Americans believe violence is ______________. Because of the emphasis ______________ competition, more importance is ______________ to men's sports than ______________. Although this is changing, ______________ people still see women ______________ cheerleaders in a traditional ______________ of supporting men. Americans ______________ view their leisure time ______________ an opportunity for self-improvement, ______________ they frequently seek recreational

________ such as running, tennis ________ skiing, which require a ________ level of physical activity. ________ and artistic activities are ________ in popularity. Handicrafts and ________ give Americans a feeling ________ self-reliance. Although Americans do ________ to rest and relax, ________ spend some of their ________ time in activities that ________ them.

E. Outlining

In this exercise you will construct an outline for the chapter. Decide whether to write a topic outline or a sentence outline and then write all entries in the same form. Do not mix complete and incomplete sentences in one outline. Be sure to put all the information into the correct form, using Roman numerals for main ideas and letters for supporting details, with Arabic numbers for further details.

I. ________
  A. ________
    1. ________
    2. ________
  B. ________
    1. ________
    2. ________
II. ________

When you list supporting details in an outline, you must always have two or more entries: if there is an A, there must be a B. If there is a 1, there must be a 2. Think of it as dividing information: if you divide something, it must be divided into at least two parts.

In previous chapters the headings for sections of the chapter have been used as the main points—the Roman numerals—of the chapter outline. How many headings are there for this chapter?

Using these headings as your Roman numerals, construct your outline section by section. Use the guide below:

Section I: **There are three main values mentioned in this section—competition, equality of opportunity, and the national religion. You may want to use these ideas as the lettered entries (A, B, C) for this section. Skim the section and find where each is presented. Remember to arrange the information in your outline in the same order in which it was presented in the chapter.**

Section II: **Which of the following is *not* a criticism of American sports found in this section?**

A. The philosophy of "winning is all"
B. The amount of money wasted on sports
C. The amount of violence in sports

Use this information in writing A and B of this section. Put these supporting details where they belong:

1. Fighting at games
2. Injuries
3. The belief in the value of competition in spite of violence in sports

Section III: **What two main points are made in this section? (Use as A and B.)**

Section IV: **This section deals with the high level of activity, the interest in self-improvement, and the interest in self-reliance evident in the ways in which many Americans spend their leisure time. (Use as A, B, and C.)**

F. Ask Yourself

How do you prefer to spend your leisure time? Read the following list of leisure-time activities and decide which things you enjoy most. Imagine that you had a whole day free and you could spend it doing any of the activities on the list. What would you most like to do? List that as number 1. Put the rest of the items in order of importance of things you would like to do on your free day.

1. Go on a hike
2. Read a good book
3. See a movie
4. Play tennis
5. Work on your car
6. Have dinner at a nice restaurant
7. Watch TV
8. Go to a friend's house
9. Have a friend visit you
10. Go swimming
11. Listen to records
12. Attend a concert
13. Have a family picnic
14. See a play
15. Visit a museum
16. Go shopping
17. Go to a game
18. Other (you name it)

G. Ask Americans

Check to see whether there are differences in the way men and women relate to sports. Ask men and women the following questions and record their answers.

1. Do you participate in sports?
2. What sports do you play?
3. How often do you play these?
4. Which do you prefer?
5. Do you attend sports events or watch them on TV?
6. If so, which are your favorites?
7. Which do you enjoy watching more, professional or amateur ball games?
8. Do you think it is important to be physically fit?
9. How do you keep fit?
10. Do you prefer to watch sports or to participate in them yourself?

What conclusions can you draw from this survey? Are there some sports that are more popular with men than with women? Do you think that Americans prefer to participate in sports or to watch them? Do they prefer team sports or individual sports?

H. Test a Hypothesis

Some people say that Americans don't have any culture. By that they probably mean that the United States has not been a country long enough to have developed its own art forms, traditions, music, dance, or theater—what we usually refer to as the fine arts.

Let's test that hypothesis. If you are living in the United States, find out about your local community. Are there libraries? Museums? Theaters where concerts and plays are performed? Check the entertainment section of your local newspaper and see if any of the following are scheduled:

1. Ballets or other dance performances
2. Plays
3. Operas
4. Art or other exhibitions
5. Lectures
6. Symphony concerts
7. Other concerts or musical performances

Are the performers or the artists Americans, or are they from another country? Are they performing works created by an American, or someone from another country? For example, if there is a play scheduled, is it being performed by American actors? Was the play written by an American playwright?

Make a list of these performances or exhibitions and indicate the nationality of both the artist who is performing the work and the artist who created it. What do you conclude?

I. Suggestions for Research

1. Sports and entertainment are the "great equalizers" in American life; that is, anyone, regardless of ethnic background, race, family status, economic status, or other factor, can rise to the top in these fields. Find examples of black entertainers and sports stars.
2. The change in women's roles in the United States has been particularly evident in sports. Decades ago women's participation in sports was limited to a few sports—tennis, golf, swimming—and the amount of attention paid to them or the amount of money that a professional woman athlete could get was very small. So was the amount of money spent on women's athletics in colleges and universities. Now much of that has changed. Have you seen any of the magazines devoted solely to women in sports? If you can, go to a local magazine stand or the library and write down the names of the magazines that deal only with women in sports. If you cannot find these, then look through a regular sports magazine such as *Sports Illustrated* or other American magazines and see whether women are mentioned in the articles on sports. If so, list the sports and the names of the athletes.
3. Look in an encyclopedia or other reference book in your library to find out how many American authors have received the Nobel Prize for Literature. Now, list their names and the titles of at least two books they wrote.
4. Look in newspapers and magazines for articles on physical fitness—jogging, running, "working out," "getting in shape." List titles of articles you find. Who is interested in physical fitness in America today?

J. Suggestions for Writing

1. American sports are one area where the seemingly contradictory values of teamwork/cooperation and individualism/competition come together. If you have an opportunity to watch an American football game, baseball game, or basketball game, describe how both of these traits are exemplified.
2. Why do you think Americans prefer their type of football to "football" (what Americans call "soccer") in most other parts of the world? What are the differences between these games? Write a brief comparison/contrast. Indicate which you prefer and why.
3. Many American social commentators have observed that the game of American football serves as a microcosm of American life; that is, many of the values Americans hold are exemplified in the game. How does football reflect the following values?

   a. Competition
   b. Teamwork
   c. Individualism and self-reliance
   d. Hard work
   e. Struggle as a means to success

K. Ask Americans

The weekend is traditionally considered the time to forget the week's work and to have fun. Many Americans even refer to their Friday night's activities as TGIF. See if you can find out what TGIF means. Ask Americans what this stands for and what it means to them.

Ask Americans to talk about what they do for fun. Then make a list of their answers and analyze them for the following:

1. Do these involve some kind of physical activity?
2. Do these involve being with friends or others?
3. Do these cost money?

THE 28-HOUR DAY

Question: I'd like you to imagine a situation in which you had four extra hours every day to do whatever you wanted to do. Which *two* or *three* of these things do you think you would do more of with those extra four hours? (Card shown respondent) . . .

Activity	Percent
Spend time on hobbies and interests	37%
Fix things around the house	36%
Read	35%
Socialize with friends	25%
Spend more time with family	24%
Exercise or play sports	21%
Put all the things I do now in better order	15%
Take a course or study something	14%
Spend time by myself	12%
Watch television	11%
Sleep	10%
Cook	8%
Put more time into present job or business	4%
Daydream and think	3%
Work at a second job	3%
Eat	2%
Other	4%
None	1%

Note: Response total adds to more than 100 percent due to multiple responses.

Source: Survey by the Roper Organization (Roper Report 78-5), April 22-May 3, 1978.

Public Opinion, August/September 1979

L. What's Your Opinion?

The physical fitness craze which began in the 1970s seems to be here to stay. It was the subject of a cover story done by *Time* magazine on November 2, 1981, "America Shapes Up." On any given day, *Time* reports, 70 million Americans will engage in some physical activity designed to get them or keep them in shape. This represents about half the adult population of the United States. In 1960 only 24 percent "worked out." Americans now spend an estimated $30 billion a year on keeping fit—sportswear, health foods and vitamins, diet and exercise books, health clubs, and fitness programs.

Some observers believe that the physical fitness craze is changing the American ideal of female beauty. This was the subject of the *Time* magazine cover story, "The New Ideal of Beauty" on August 30, 1982. Women are now reshaping their bodies through exercise and weight lifting.

> At home or on the beach or by the office water cooler, a new form is emerging. It may be slimmer than before, but it is surely stronger. It may be massive or petite, but it is always graceful.

American women who work out say they do it because it makes them feel good and it raises their self-confidence. Most American women like the new look. Some men like it and some don't. What's your opinion?

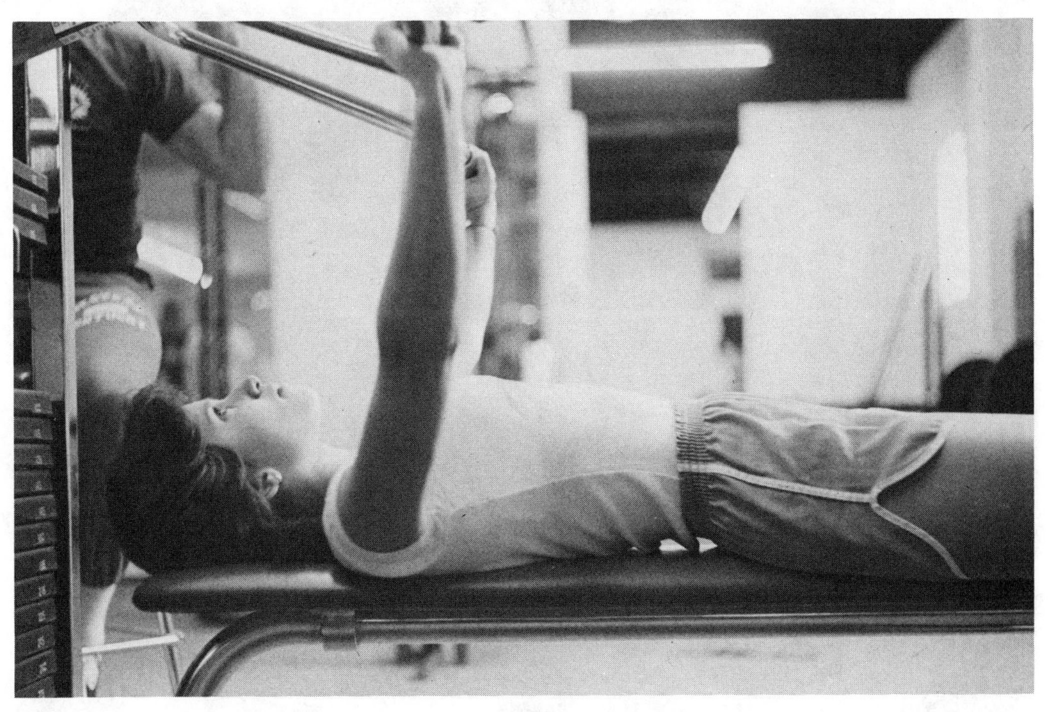

Bill Jackson.

M. Suggestions for Further Reading

Jim Bouton. *Ball Four.*
Jerry Kramer and Dick Schaap. *Instant Replay.*
George Plimpton. *The Paper Lion.*
Michael Novak. *The Joy of Sports.*
J. W. Lory, Jr., and G. S. Kenyon, Eds. *Sport, Culture and Society.*
Ernest Hemingway. "The Short, Happy Life of Francis Macomber".

Radio Shack, a division of Tandy Corp.

chapter 11

The American Family

The American has fashioned anew the features of his family institutions, as he does everything else about him.

Max Lerner

A Middle Eastern student returned home to teach at a state university. He was offered positions at three universities and had to decide which one to accept. An American friend who was visiting him in Iran noticed that the man's older brother had accompanied him to all the interviews at the universities, and she asked him about it. The man, who was nearly 40, explained that he would follow the advice of his brother in choosing the position. "But why?" asked the American in amazement. "Oh," the student replied, "because he is the head of the family now, and I must do whatever he thinks will be best for the family."

The Emphasis on Individual Freedom

The American was surprised that the student did not feel free to choose his own career but instead thought first about what would be best for the family. In a similar situation an American man or woman would expect to decide what job would be best for himself or herself as an individual. Indeed, young Americans are encouraged by their families to make such independent career decisions. What would be best for the family is not considered to be as important as what would be best for the individual.

Americans view the family as a group whose primary purpose is to advance the happiness of individual members. The result is that the needs of each individual take **priority** in the life of the family. In contrast to that of many other cultures, the primary responsibility of the American family member is not to advance the family as a group, either socially or economically, nor to bring honor to the family name. This is partly because the United States is not an aristocratic society.

Family name and honor are less important than in aristocratic societies, since equality of opportunity regardless of birth is considered a basic American value. Moreover, there is less emphasis on the family as an economic unit because the American family is rarely self-supporting. Relatively few families maintain self-supporting family farms or businesses for more than one generation. A farmer's son, for example, is very likely to go on to college, leave the family farm, and take an entirely different job in a different location.

The American desire for freedom from outside control clearly extends to the family. Americans do not like to have controls placed on them by other family members. They want to make independent decisions and not be told what to do by grandparents or uncles or aunts.

The American family is a nuclear family, consisting usually of a husband, wife, and children who live in their own house or apartment. Grandparents rarely live in the same home with their married sons and daughters, and uncles and aunts almost never do. Americans have fewer children than in many other cultures. The typical American couple has two children, so that the average American family has four people living together as a household unit. A great value is placed on each child's having a room of his or her own.

If Americans are asked to name the members of their families, family structure becomes clear. Married American adults will name their husband or wife and their children, if they have any, as their "immediate family." If they mention their father, mother, sisters, or brothers, they will define them as separate units, usually living in separate households. Aunts, uncles, cousins, and grandparents are considered "extended family."

Marriage and Divorce

Marriages are not "arranged" in the United States. Young people are expected to find a husband or wife on their own; their parents do not help them. In fact, parents are frequently not told of marriage plans until the couple has decided to marry. This means that parents have little control, and generally not much influence, over whom their children marry. Americans believe that young people should fall in love and then decide to marry someone they can live happily with, again evidence of the importance of an individual's happiness. Of course, in reality this does not always happen, but it remains the ideal and it shapes the views of **courtship** and marriage among young Americans.

Tom Hughes.

Over the years the value placed on marriage itself is determined largely by how happy the husband and wife make each other. Happiness is based primarily on companionship. The majority of American women value companionship as the most important part of marriage. Other values, such as having economic support and the opportunity to have children, although important, are seen as less important.

If the couple is not happy, the individuals may choose to get a divorce. A divorce is relatively easy to obtain in most parts of the United States. Some states have "no-fault" divorce. To obtain a no-fault divorce, a couple states that they can no longer live happily together, that they have "**irreconcilable differences**," and that it is neither partner's fault.

The divorce rate has risen rapidly in the United States over the last twenty years. Approximately one out of every three marriages ends in divorce, and the numbers are rising. Often children are involved. The great majority of adult Americans believe that unhappy couples should not stay married for the sake of the children, which is a significant change in attitude. Until recently, most

Americans believed that couples with children at home should stay together at least until the children were grown. They would sacrifice individual happiness for the sake of the children. The current generation, however, defends its view with the argument that unhappy marriages do not contribute to the happiness of the children.

The Role of the Child

The emphasis on the individual rather than the group finds expression in other ways. American families tend to place more emphasis on the needs and desires of the child and less on social and family responsibilities. In the years since World War II, so much stress has been placed on the psychological needs of children that the number of experts in this field has increased enormously. Child psychologists, **counselors**, and social workers are employed to help children with problems at school or in the family. Many books on how to raise children have become best sellers. Sometimes these books offer conflicting advice, but almost all of them share the American emphasis on the development of the individual as their primary goal.

In the 1970s some Americans concluded that the emphasis on the psychological needs of the individual child had been carried too far by parents and experts alike. Dr. Benjamin Spock, the most famous of the child-rearing experts, wrote in 1973 that his outlook had changed since his best-selling handbook, *Baby and Child Care*, was first published in 1945. He had come to the conclusion that "what is making the parent's job most difficult is today's child-centered viewpoint." Many **conscientious** parents, said Spock, tend to "keep their eyes exclusively focused on their child, thinking about what he needs from them and from the community, instead of thinking about what the world, the neighborhood, the family will be needing from the child and then making sure that he will grow up to meet such obligations."

Although Americans may be changing some of their attitudes, they still hold the basic belief that the major purpose of the family is the development and welfare of each of its members as individuals.

Equality in the Family

Along with the American emphasis on individual freedom, the belief in equality has had a strong effect on the family. Alexis de Tocqueville saw the connection clearly in the 1830s. He said that in aristocratic societies inequality extends into the family, particularly to the father's relationship to his children. The father is accepted as ruler and master. The children's relations with him are very formal, and love for him is always combined with fear. In the United States, however, the democratic idea of equality destroys much of the father's status as ruler of the family and lessens the emotional distance between father and children. There is less formal respect for, and fear of, the father. But there is more affection expressed toward him. "The master and **constituted** ruler have **vanished**," said Tocqueville; "the father remains."

What Tocqueville said of American fathers and children a century and a half ago applies to relations between parents and children in the United States today. There is much more social equality between parents and children than in most aristocratic societies or societies ruled by centuries of tradition. This can be witnessed in dinner table arguments or debates between parents and their children, or in the considerable independence granted to teenagers. In fact, most Americans are worried that there is too much democracy in the home. The last twenty years have seen a significant decline in parental authority and children's respect for their parents. This is particularly true of teenagers. Some parents seem to have little or no control over the behavior of their teenage children.

Ken Karp.

Four Stages of Marriage Relationships

The idea of equality also affects the relationships between husbands and wives. Women have witnessed steady progress toward equal status for themselves in the family and in society at large. According to Letha and John Scanzoni, two

American sociologists, the institution of marriage in the United States has experienced four stages of development.* In each new stage, wives have increased the degree of equality with their husbands and have gained more power within the family.

Stage I: Wife as Servant to Husband During the nineteenth century American wives were expected to be completely obedient to their husbands. As late as 1850, wife beating was legal in almost all the states of the United States. Although both husbands and wives had family duties, the wife had no power in family matters other than that which her husband allowed her. Her possessions and any of her earnings belonged to her husband. During the nineteenth century women were not allowed to vote, a restriction that in part reflected women's status as servant to the family.

Stage II: Husband-Head, Wife-Helper During the late nineteenth and early twentieth centuries opportunities for women to work outside the household increased. More wives were now able to support themselves, if necessary, and therefore were less likely to accept the traditional idea that wives were servants who must obey their husbands. Even though the great majority of wives chose not to work outside the home, the fact that they might do so increased their power in the marriage. The husband could no longer make family decisions alone and demand that the wife follow them. The wife was freer to disagree with her husband and to insist that her views be taken into account in family decisions.

Even though the wife's power increased, the husband remained the head of the family. The wife became his full-time helper by taking care of his house and raising his children. She might strongly argue with him and sometimes convince him, but his decision on family matters was usually final.

This increase in equality of women in marriages reflected increased status for women in the society at large and led to women's gaining the right to vote in the early twentieth century.

The husband-head, wife-helper marriage is still frequently found in the United States. Economic conditions in the twentieth century, however, have carried many marriages into different stages.

Stage III: Husband-Senior Partner, Wife-Junior Partner During the twentieth century more and more wives have taken jobs outside the home. In 1940, for example, only 14 percent of married women in the United States held jobs outside the home. By 1980 more than 50 percent did so. When married

* Scanzoni, Letha D. and John Scanzoni, *Men, Women, and Change*, McGraw-Hill, Inc. 1981.

women take this step, according to Scanzoni, their power relative to that of their husbands increases still further. The wife's income becomes important in maintaining the family's standard of living. Her power to affect the outcome of family decisions is greater than when her duties were entirely in the home.

Although she has become a partner, however, she is still not an equal partner with her husband, since his job or career still provides most of the family income. He is therefore, the senior partner and she is the junior partner of the family enterprise. Even though she has a job, it has a lower priority than her husband's. If, for example, the husband is asked to move to advance his career, she will give up her job and seek another in a new location.

In the United States today most marriages are either the husband-head or the husband-senior partner type, but the latter is becoming more typical as more and more wives take jobs outside the home. This is due partly to the desire of American women for greater economic opportunity, but the main reason seems to be that in the last ten years it has become increasingly difficult for families to maintain their standard of living in the face of rising inflation and declining abundance. Most American families simply cannot **make ends meet** on just one income. More than any other factor, the need to maintain a good standard of living is making the husband-senior partner, wife-junior partner the typical form of American marriage.

Stage IV: Husband-Wife Equal Partners Since the late 1960s a growing number of women have expressed a strong dissatisfaction with any marriage arrangement wherein the husband and his career are the primary considerations in the marriage. By the end of the 1970s, for example, considerably less than half of the women in the United States (38 percent) still believed that they should put their husbands and children ahead of their own careers.

More and more American women have come to believe that they should be equal partners rather than junior partners in their marriages. According to Scanzoni, this fourth stage of marriage, although not typical of most American marriages at present, will grow most rapidly in the future.

In an equal partnership marriage, the wife pursues a full-time job or career which has equal importance to her husband's. The long-standing division of labor between husband and wife comes to an end. The husband is no longer the main provider of family income, and the wife no longer has the main responsibilities for household duties and raising children. Husband and wife share all these duties equally. Power over family decisions is also shared equally.

The rapid change in women's attitudes toward marriage in the 1970s reflected rapid change in the larger society. The Women's Liberation movement appeared in the late 1960s, demanding an end to all forms of sexual discrimination against females. An Equal Rights Amendment to the U.S. Constitution was proposed which would make any form of discrimination on the basis of sex illegal, and though it has failed to be ratified, it continues to have millions of supporters.

A telephone company cable splicer. Many women are now seeking jobs traditionally held by men. *A.T.&T. Co. Photo Center.*

The Role of the Family in Society

The American ideal of equality has affected not only marriage but all forms of relationships between men and women. Americans gain a number of benefits by placing great importance on achieving individual freedom and equality within the context of the family. The needs and desires of each member are given a great deal of attention and importance. However, a price is paid for these benefits. American families are less **stable** and lasting than those of most cultures. The high rate of divorce in American families is perhaps the most important indicator of this instability.

The American attitude toward the family contains many contradictions. For example, Americans will tolerate a good deal of instability in their families, including divorce, in order to protect such values as freedom and equality. On the other hand, they are strongly attached to the idea of the family as the best of all lifestyles. A recent survey showed that 78 percent of Americans felt that the family was the most meaningful part of life and 92 percent said it was a very important personal value to them. In fact, the great majority of persons who get divorces find a new partner and remarry.

Some social scientists have explained this apparent contradiction in an interesting way. Americans, they say, look upon the family as a necessary **refuge** from the competitive world outside. As we have seen in previous chapters, competition and hard work are basic American values, but they also place a psychological strain on the individual. By contrast, the family is basically a noncompetitive, cooperative institution. Family members are not expected to compete against each other as they do against their peers in the outside worlds of business, politics, and education. Rather, the ideal of the American family is group cooperation to help achieve the fulfillment of each individual member, and shared affection to renew each member's emotional strength.

Families can be viewed as similar to churches in this regard. Both are seen by Americans as places where the human spirit can find refuge from the highly competitive world outside and renewed resources to continue the effort. Although in many cases churches and families do not succeed in the task of spiritual renewal, such remains the ideal of church and family in America.

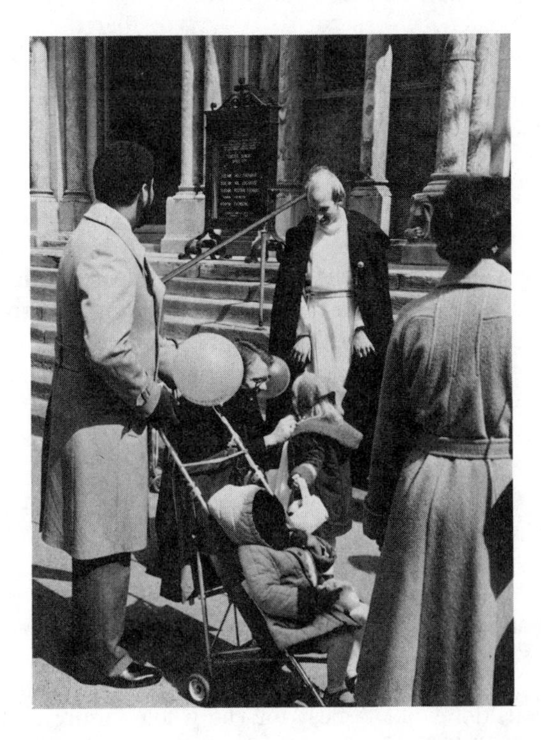

Ken Karp.

New Words

priority position of most importance; matter having first place

courtship the time two people spend deciding if they want to marry

irreconcilable differences differences over which people cannot agree; different opinions to the extent that people cannot solve their problems

counselor a person who has studied psychology and is trained to help people with their personal problems

conscientious trying hard to do the right thing

constituted established, legal

vanish to disappear completely

make ends meet to earn enough money to pay expenses

stable firm and strong; unchanging

refuge a safe place

A. Vocabulary Check

Write the letter of the correct definition next to each word.

____ 1. conscientious
____ 2. constituted
____ 3. counselor
____ 4. courtship
____ 5. irreconcilable differences
____ 6. make ends meet
____ 7. priority
____ 8. refuge
____ 9. stable
____ 10. vanish

a. to disappear completely
b. firm and strong; unchanging
c. established; legal
d. a safe place
e. position having most importance
f. opinions over which people are not able to agree
g. trying hard to do the right thing
h. the time spent deciding whether or not to marry
i. someone who helps people with their problems
j. to earn enough money to pay expenses

B. Comprehension Check

Write T if the statement is true and F if it is false according to the information in the chapter.

____ 1. Americans usually consider what is best for the whole family first and what is best for them as individuals second.

____ 2. Americans believe that the family exists primarily to serve the needs of its individual family members.

____ 3. Most Americans would define a family unit or household as consisting of parents and their children.

____ 4. Most Americans believe that marriages should make both individuals happy and that if they cannot live together happily, it is better for them to get a divorce.

____ 5. American parents generally think more about the individual needs of their children than they do about what responsibilities the child will have to the society as a whole.

____ 6. Although Americans believe in democracy for society, they generally exercise strict control over their children, particularly teenagers.

____ 7. The amount of equality between husbands and wives has remained pretty much the same for the last 150 years.

____ 8. If an American wife works outside the home, she is likely to have more power in the family than a married woman who does not hold a job.

____ 9. In the husband–senior partner, wife–junior partner type of marriage, the husband and wife both work, have equal power and influence in making family decisions, and divide the family duties equally between them.

____ 10. Although the divorce rate in the United States is very high, Americans still believe strongly in marriage and the family.

C. Questions for Discussion or Composition

1. What is the ideal purpose of the American family? What is the ideal purpose of the family in your country?
2. Why are American families relatively small? How large is your family? Is this the average size of families in your country? What do you think is the ideal number of children to have?
3. Should the family exist to serve the needs of its individual members? What responsibilities and obligations do individuals have to their families in your country? Whose needs should come first, the parents' or the children's?
4. How much democracy is there in the family in your country? How much freedom do teenagers have? How much should they have?
5. What are the four types of marriage described by Scanzoni? Which type is best for the wife? Which type is best for the husband? Which type of marriage do you want for yourself? Why? Is this the "ideal" type?
6. What are the grounds for divorce in your country? What happens to people who divorce there? How are they treated? Do they usually remarry? If two people are unhappy, should they get a divorce? What if they have children? Under what circumstances would you get a divorce?
7. The chapter says that most American women value companionship as the most important part of marriage. Do you agree or disagree? What are some other

reasons for getting married? List them and rank them in order of importance. Explain your choices.

8. Should married women work? What if they have small children? Who should take care of the children? Are there day care centers for children of working mothers in your country? Do other members of the family (grandmothers, aunts, etc.) care for children? Would you leave your child with a sitter or at a day care center?

D. Cloze Summary Paragraph

This paragraph summarizes the chapter. Fill in each blank with any word that makes sense.

Americans believe that the ___*primary*___ purpose of the family ______________ to advance the happiness ______________ individual family members. Family ______________ are small and are ______________ limited to parents and ______________ children. The stress on ______________ happiness means that (1) unhappy ______________ frequently end in divorce, ______________ (2) more emphasis is placed ______________ the needs of the ______________ than on the child's ______________ to others. The American ______________ in equality results in ______________ democratic relationships within the ______________, both between parents and ______________ and between husbands and ______________. American marriages have progressed ______________ four stages, from the ______________ as servant, to the ______________ as a completely equal ______________ with her husband. The ______________ of the wife within ______________ family and the degree ______________ her equality with her ______________ have increased as women ______________ taken jobs outside the ______________. The emphasis on individual ______________ and equality has caused ______________ high divorce rate in ______________ United States, but Americans ______________ value marriage and the ______________ as a necessary refuge ______________ their competitive society.

E. Ask Americans

Interview at least three Americans of different ages (one under 21, one middle-aged, and one over 60) and ask them about their families. Ask each one the following questions and record their answers.

1. Who are the members of your family? Name them and indicate their relationship to you (mother, sister, etc.).
2. Who lives in your household? Where do your other relatives live?
3. How often do you see your parents? Your grandparents? Your sisters and brothers? Your aunts, uncles, and cousins? Do you write or telephone any of them regularly?
4. What occasions bring your relatives together (birthdays, holidays, weddings, births, deaths, trips)? Have you ever been to a family reunion?
5. Do you feel you have a close family? Why?
6. Who would you ask for advice if you had a serious personal problem?
7. Who would take care of you if you became ill?
8. What obligations and responsibilities do you feel you have toward your family?
9. What duties and responsibilities does a child have to its family?
10. On a scale of 1 to 10, with 10 as "most important," how important are the opinions of the members of your immediate family concerning:
    Whom you marry
    Where you live
    Where you go to school
    What job you take
    How you spend your money

F. Ask Yourself

Do you agree or disagree with each of the statements below? Put a check under the number that indicates how you feel.

+2 = Strongly agree
+1 = Agree
0 = No opinion
−1 = Disagree
−2 = Strongly disagree

	+2	+1	0	−1	−2
1. Arranged marriages are better than marriages where the couple have met and dated on their own.	___	___	___	___	___
2. It is very important for my family to approve of the person I marry.	___	___	___	___	___
3. If my parents disapproved of my choice, I would not marry that person even if we were very much in love.	___	___	___	___	___
4. A woman's place is in the home.	___	___	___	___	___
5. Married women with small children should not work.	___	___	___	___	___
6. Some women are better mothers if they work and are not with their children all day.	___	___	___	___	___
7. Children should be spanked if they misbehave.	___	___	___	___	___
8. Parents should put the needs of their children before their own personal needs.	___	___	___	___	___
9. Children should put the needs of their families before their own personal needs.	___	___	___	___	___
10. Equality between a husband and wife causes divorce.	___	___	___	___	___

Now, if you have an American friend or acquaintance, ask him or her to do the same. Compare your answers.

G. Outlining

There are two main values which are used as themes in this chapter: individual freedom and equality. Instead of looking at each chapter heading as a separate Roman numeral, we might outline the chapter using these two points as the Roman numeral entries:

I. The emphasis on individual freedom
  A. The structure of the American family
  B. Marriage and divorce
  C. The role of the child

II. Equality in the family
  A. Parental authority
  B. Four stages of marriage relationships
  C. The role of the family in society

Skim the chapter to find these main points, and then recopy the outline and provide supporting details (1,2,3, etc.) for each of the lettered entries. Be sure to use phrases and *not* complete sentences, since this is a topic outline.

H. People Watching

It has been said that in most societies children are spectators watching adults interact. They are learning what it means to be an adult in their society. In American society, however, the adults are usually the spectators who are watching the children.

Observe American adults interacting with children in the following places.

In restaurants
On a playground or at a sports event
At the movies
On the street
At home (If you are not able to visit an American home, watch American TV shows that have children as characters.)

Record your observations. You may wish to write up these observations as a report and present it to the class. What differences did you observe from the way children are treated in other countries?

I. Suggestions for Research

The concept of the "ideal" family may differ considerably from the reality of the average family. What people think the ideal family should be and what the average family really is may be quite different.

Write a comparison/contrast essay on this subject, choosing from the topics below.

1. The Ideal Family Versus the Average Family in the United States
2. The Ideal Family Versus the Average Family in My Country
3. The Ideal American Family Versus the Ideal Family in My Country
4. The Average American Family Versus the Average Family in My Country

Use several methods of research. Go to the library and find current statistics and articles on your topic. You may wish to find statistics on (1) the size of the average family, (2) how many single parents there are (divorced or widowed), (3) how many married women work, (4) how many women with small children work, and (5) a comparison of the average income for working men and women. Conduct interviews and ask people to fill in the following chart.

	Ideal Family	***Average Family***
1. How many children are there?		
2. Do children leave home after they grow up?		
3. Do the grandparents live with their children and grandchildren?		
4. How often do families get together? On what occasions?		
5. Does the wife work?		
6. Does the mother of small children work?		

J. Ask Americans

The role of the elderly is one that most foreigners cannot understand about American life. To try to understand how Americans feel about being old and what they plan to do with their lives when they are old, ask several Americans who are not yet 65 the following questions:

1. What do you hope to do when you retire?
2. Where do you plan to live?
3. Would you move in with your children? Under what conditions?
4. What do you think life will be like when you are 65 or older?
5. Are you afraid of growing old? Are you looking forward to growing old?

If you are able to, you may wish to visit a retirement community for older Americans, or a nursing home. Why are many older people living apart from their grown children? Think about the description of the family presented in this chapter. What evidence do you see of the American values of equality in the family and the emphasis on individual freedom?

Ken Karp, Sirovich Senior Center.

K. Proverbs and Sayings

Ask Americans to explain these proverbs and sayings to you. Then ask them for other examples of sayings about men, women, children or the family.

1. The hand that rocks the cradle rules the world.
2. As the twig is bent, so grows the tree.
3. That child is a chip off the old block.
4. A man may work from sun to sun, but a woman's work is never done.
5. Behind every successful man, there is a woman.
6. Blood is thicker than water.

L. What's Your Opinion?

Working mothers often feel that they have two full-time jobs—one outside the home, for which they get paid, and the other inside the home, for which they do not get paid. The job at home is being "household manager." Most working American women still have the major responsibility for managing the household—cooking, cleaning, shopping, and seeing that the children are cared for—even if their husbands help them with some of the household duties. What do you think husbands with working wives should do around the house? Should married women work? What if they have children?

M. Have a Debate

How do you feel about couples who decide they never want children? Are they selfish and immature or is this a mature personal decision that is the best choice for some couples?

Prepare to debate the topic: "Married Couples Should/Should Not Be Expected to Have Children." Be sure to list the points you wish to make before you begin the debate. Have the class vote to decide which team wins.

CONSIDER THE COST OF KIDS

Question: I'm going to read you a list of rules people used to believe were important to families and family life, but which people now feel are old-fashioned and out-of-date. Will you tell me for each one whether this is something you personally still believe in completely, partially, or no longer believe in? . . . Married couples should not have children if they cannot afford them.

Source: Survey by *Time*/Yankelovich, Skelly and White, March 1978.

Public Opinion, December/January 1980

OK TO CONSIDER YOURSELF, TOO

Question: (Hand respondent two sets of cards)* Once again, we have a group of cards, each one containing a statement. Would you please read each statement, call off its identification letter, and then the number of the item on the scale card EE that best describes the extent of your agreement or disagreement with the statement. . . . Married couples who choose not to have children are basically selfish.

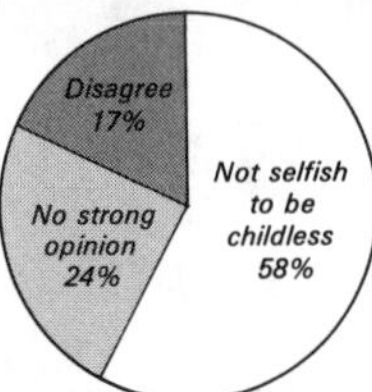

Note: *Respondent given one set of cards with various statements and another card with possible response categories. Agree =Agree strongly and Agree; Disagree = Disagree and Disagree strongly; No strong opinion = Not sure, but probably agree and Not sure, but probably disagree.

Source: Survey by Yankelovich, Skelly and White conducted for the American Council of Life Insurance, May 19-June 15, 1978.

N. Suggestions for Writing

It is sometimes difficult for young people to find someone to marry. Young adults are expected to find their own husbands or wives themselves, but it is often difficult for them to meet others, especially if they are not in college. Families play a very minor role in getting young people together. Some young adults have turned to computer dating or putting advertisements in the newspapers. These new services are designed to help people meet "Mr. or Miss Right." Men and women are asked to fill out questionnaires about themselves—their interests, hobbies, likes and dislikes—and they also indicate the qualities they are looking for in a husband or wife. Couples are then matched by the computer, and each person receives a list of names of people to contact for a date.

Imagine that you are writing an ad for the newspaper, or explaining to a computer service what kind of person you would like to meet (and perhaps marry). What things about yourself would be important for your date to know? What qualities would you want your date to have?

Write an ad describing yourself and the kind of person you would like to meet, *or* choose one of the composition topics below.

1. Qualities I Want My Husband/Wife to Have
2. The Pros and Cons of Computer Dating
3. How to Find the Perfect Mate
4. Courtship in My Country
5. The Real Me

O. Suggestions for Further Reading

Letha and John Scanzoni. *Men, Women and Change.*
Laura Ingalls Wilder. *Little House on the Prairie.*
Louisa May Alcott. *Little Women.*
Tennessee Williams. *The Glass Menagerie.*
Thornton Wilder. *Our Town.*
Willa Cather. *My Antonia.*
Robert S. and Helen M. Lynd. *Middletown.*
Betty Friedan. *The Feminine Mystique.*

The Washington Post.

The Vietnam Veterans' Memorial in Washington, D.C. *UPI*.

chapter 12

American Values at the Crossroads

The erosion of our confidence in the future is threatening to destroy the social and political fabric of America.... The symptoms of this crisis of the American spirit are all around us.

Former President Jimmy Carter

President Carter's words, delivered in a televised address to the nation in July 1979, were perhaps the **gloomiest** statement about the American spirit ever made by a President to the American people. Many observers felt that Carter had greatly **exaggerated** the decline of the American spirit. Many others, however, had been reporting a decline in the faith of Americans in their future, in their institutions, and even in many of their values since the 1960s.

The Challenge to American Values

Surely, Americans had experienced a number of things which had caused them to be more doubtful about the strength of their nation and its basic values. A popular President, John F. Kennedy, had been assassinated in 1963. After his death, the nation under President Johnson vastly increased the number of American troops in the Southeast Asian country of Vietnam. Johnson did this in order to prevent the Vietnamese communists from taking control of the country. He believed that communism would spread throughout Southeast Asia if it succeeded in Vietnam. By 1966, the struggle in Vietnam had become a major American war.

Most Americans agreed with the action. But even so, there was stronger opposition to the Vietnam War than to any previous American war in the twentieth century. Most of the opponents of the war attacked it as immoral. They believed it was immoral for the United States to try to determine the future of a distant country by means of war. Many opponents of the Vietnam war also attacked the nation's basic values as corrupt. Some of the harshest criticism of the United States and its values by American citizens was heard during this period of protest against the war.

While most Americans strongly rejected this harsh criticism of their nation's values, some observers believe that the anti-war movement made many Americans who supported the war more doubtful about their beliefs. An even greater blow to the majority who supported the war was the fact that the United States failed in its objective. The purpose of the war was to protect an ally of the United States, South Vietnam, against defeat at the hands of the communist North Vietnam. More than half a million American soldiers were sent to achieve this purpose, but this was not enough. Rather than send even more soldiers to Vietnam or take the dangerous step of using nuclear weapons, the United States began to bring its soldiers home in 1969.

In 1975 North Vietnam conquered South Vietnam. The result was discouraging to all Americans. The opponents of the war continued to feel that the nation had done something terribly immoral. The people who had supported the war were discouraged by its outcome. Most Americans had been brought up believing that the United States had never lost a war. Now it seemed that for the first time, this had happened. Was the nation losing its strength? If it was, was this because it was losing faith in its basic values? These were the kinds of troubling questions Vietnam raised in the minds of many Americans.

Before the Vietnam War was ended, the Watergate scandals involving the next President, Richard Nixon, dealt a second major blow to the confidence Americans had in their nation and its values. Because the President of the United States is supposed to be an outstanding example of the nation's values, the scandals tended to weaken the faith of many Americans in these values. President Nixon was forced to resign from office in 1974. Three aspects of the affair made it the most serious scandal in American history. First, illegal **sabotage** and **espionage** activities on a large scale were carried out by agents and associates of the President against his leading political opponents in the United States. Men paid by President Nixon's reelection committee were arrested for breaking into the national headquarters of the opposition Democratic party (in the Watergate building) in order to place illegal listening devices on the telephones and to photograph party documents. Second, the President used all the powers of his office to keep law **enforcement** officials from finding out the truth about these activities. Third, he repeatedly lied to the American people, claiming to be innocent of all wrongdoing even after the American people had ceased to believe him.

Before the Watergate scandal, American Presidents, even unpopular ones, were thought to be basically honest, **law-abiding** men. President Nixon's conduct in office weakened the faith and respect Americans held for their presidents. Faith in American values was also weakened because of the belief that the President is the nation's first citizen and the most important defender of its values. "If you can't trust the President, who can you trust?" was the question on the minds of many.

The failure of the Vietnam War effort and the resignation of President Nixon in **disgrace** did not destroy the faith of Americans in their values, but the faith seems to have been weakened by these events. After Vietnam and Watergate, a third development appeared, which threatened to weaken the faith even further. This was the possibility that for the first time since the Great Depression of the 1930s the standard of living of the American people might decline significantly. As noted in Chapter 5, the material abundance of the United States has served as a kind of sustaining food which has kept American values alive and strong. Americans have considered their high standard of living a reward for practicing their basic beliefs in individual freedom, competition, and other values. The possibility of a significant decline in living standards during the 1980s and beyond, therefore, could present a danger to the continuing strength of these values.

In the early 1980s the rate of inflation fell, but the rate of unemployment rose to over 10% in some areas. *UPI.*

In the late 1970s Americans became aware that the era of cheap and abundant energy was ending. In the 1980s Americans also began to discover that the nation's water supplies were declining at a rapid rate and that the amount of land available for farming was also declining as more and more farmland was changed into business and residential neighborhoods. These and other facts pointed to a decline in the foundations of material abundance that the United States had enjoyed throughout its history.

Political events such as Vietnam and Watergate, and probably even more important, the fear that the nation's material abundance may be declining, seem to have made Americans less optimistic about the future of their country. Two experts on American public opinion, Daniel Yankelovich and Bernard Lefkowitz, came to this conclusion after studying the results of American public opinion polls dating back to the 1950s. They observed that during the decade of the 1970s a significant change had taken place "from an optimistic faith in an open unlimited future to a fear of instability and a new sense of limits."*

Because the optimism and continuing abundance which had characterized the United States appeared to be less certain by the end of the 1970s, the basic American values which have been strengthened by them may have reached a crossroads in the 1980s.

A Return to the Past

Faced with rapid change and the fear and uncertainty that go with it, individuals as well as nations sometimes seek to return to the ways of the past as a solution. In the early 1980s the idea of returning to the ways of the past had a strong appeal to many Americans who increasingly viewed their past as being better than their future. Yankelovich and Lefkowitz have observed that until the 1970s Americans generally believed that the present was a better time for their country than the past and that the future would be better than the present; by 1978, however, public opinion polls showed that many Americans had come to believe that just the opposite was true: the past had been better for the country than the present, and the present was better than the future would be.

The popular appeal of returning to the ways of the past as a solution to the problems of the 1980s was demonstrated when Ronald Reagan was elected President of the United States in 1980. *Time* magazine chose President Reagan as its "man of the year" and said of him: "intellectually, emotionally, Reagan lives in the past."

One of President Reagan's basic beliefs is that the United States should return as much as possible to its pre-1930 ways. In those times business institutions were strong and government institutions were weak. Reagan believes that the American values of individual freedom and competition are strengthened

* *Public Opinion*, December/January 1980, p. 46.

by business and weakened by government. Therefore, his programs as President have been designed to greatly strengthen business and reduce the size and power of the national government. By moving in this way toward the practices of the past, President Reagan believed that the standard of living of Americans would begin to improve once more in the 1980s as it had done throughout most of the nation's history.

The Need for New National Values

A number of leaders in politics, education, and the professions take a different approach than does President Reagan. They believe that the nation must adopt new values to go along with the old values and that it must be prepared to make some changes in the old values when necessary.

What new values should be adopted? This is a very difficult question to answer. However, it became clear in the 1970s that there was no longer an abundance of cheap energy and that shortages of other essential resources such as water were becoming more serious. These facts suggested to many Americans that a greater value be placed on the conservation of natural resources, that is, that Americans should save more of these resources by learning to use less and waste less.

Conservation has never been a strong American value. Because of the vast resources and space of North America, Americans came to believe that abundance was endless. In such an environment, there seemed to be little need for conservation of resources. After World War II Americans believed that their modern technology could work wonders and provide a never-ending increase in their standard of living. It is not surprising, therefore, that in the United States before the 1980s, conservation had little importance compared with such other values as freedom, equality of opportunity, hard work, and the accumulation of material wealth.

There is some evidence that the experience of greater shortages of energy during the 1970s caused Americans to place more emphasis on conservation. For example, a poll taken at the end of the decade showed that 66 percent of Americans agreed with the statement: "I'm not that unhappy about the possibility of shortages because I know it will encourage me to use everything efficiently and not wastefully."*

Yankelovich and Lefkowitz, however, believe that poll results like these reveal only part of the truth. Although Americans may agree with statements supporting the value of conservation, most of them are not yet applying these beliefs in their day-to-day actions.

Belief in conservation, therefore, is still weak compared with other American beliefs. It can become stronger only as Americans see the need for it more and

* *Public Opinion*, December/January 1980, p. 52.

A.T.&T. Photo Service Center.

more clearly. Conservation may well be a new value which needs to be added to the old basic values in order to help the United States deal with its future problems.

A second belief which has never been strong among the American people is a belief in the value of cooperation on a national scale to achieve some important national objectives. The American idea of the national good has never been based on national cooperation but rather on the freedom of the individual. Americans, therefore, tend to think of the national good in terms of maintaining those conditions that provide the greatest freedom for the individual. They believe that a nation of free individuals will be naturally strong and prosperous. Planned efforts at national cooperation, therefore, are not needed. More important, planned efforts at national cooperation would mean increasing the powers of the national government, which would endanger the freedom of the individual.

The American value of competition also hinders the development of a spirit of national cooperation. This ideal often encourages Americans to work against each other. Even though competitive activity is supposed to be conducted according to fair rules, it does not encourage a spirit of cooperation. Rather, it sometimes encourages a spirit of **mutual** suspicion of the motives of others. A certain degree of trust in the motives of others is necessary for the success of efforts in national cooperation.

In time of war Americans have temporarily put aside their dislike of planned national cooperation. They have been willing to cooperate and make personal sacrifices under the direction of the national government to bring the war to a satisfactory conclusion. In peacetime, however, planned national cooperation is strongly resisted as a threat to individual freedom.

The almost unique American historical experience gives us a deeper understanding of this attitude. Almost every nation in the world has had, or still has, the experience of being ruled by kings, emperors, dictators, or a hereditary class of aristocrats. Such rulers are not elected by the free votes of the people and they have the power to say what the national good is and to force their people to cooperate if they cannot persuade them to do so. Out of these experiences there have developed traditions and habits of cooperation, sometimes for good purposes and sometimes for evil purposes.

Americans have never had the experience of being forced to cooperate on a national scale by nonelected rulers. For a time, they were the colonists of Great Britain and were legally bound to obey rulers in England whom they did not elect, but the British government allowed the colonists a great deal of freedom and self-government by the standards of the day. Still the American colonists were not long in demanding more freedom and self-government, and finally declaring their independence in 1776. From the time of their independence, Americans have freely elected their rulers. The experience of being compelled to cooperate by unelected national leaders is completely foreign to their experience. They are fearful that any scheme of national cooperation in peacetime will weaken or destroy their freedoms.

Americans have always viewed cooperation as important in small groups such as the family, the neighborhood, or the church. But on the large national scale where government becomes involved, it is seen as **coercive** and destructive rather than voluntary and constructive. Americans tend to associate the greatness of their nation far more with such values as individual freedom, equality of opportunity, hard work, and competition than with national cooperation.

Yet the demands of the 1980s may compel Americans to place a greater value on national cooperation. It may well be that some of the problems facing them, such as scarcity of resources and the dangers of air and water pollution, cannot be solved without a greater degree of national cooperation.

Drilling for oil on the ocean floor.

What of the Future?

If Americans choose to give more emphasis to national cooperation, they will probably be very cautious about it. In order to protect their freedoms, they will move slowly in a step-by-step, problem-by-problem fashion, rather than accept a sweeping new plan involving dramatic change. Because of their tradition of self-government, they will probably insist on a good deal of public discussion before any single step toward national cooperation is taken.

Some observers believe that this slow, cautious approach may be too weak and too **timid** to meet the challenges of the future. Americans, however, believe that sudden revolutionary changes made in the name of the national good usually result in dictatorships in which freedom is lost and problems remain unsolved.

In the 1980s Americans may have arrived at a critical point in their nation's history, where major dangers must be faced and major choices must be made. On the one hand, they will wish to avoid the risk of making too many changes in the basic values which have inspired them in the past. On the other hand, they must avoid what may be the greater risk of refusing to change their values at all even though conditions are changing rapidly all around them. The events of the past two decades have brought the American people and their basic values to a crossroads in their history. The last two decades of the twentieth century will determine where they will go from there.

New Words

gloomy dark; with little hope or cheerfulness
exaggerate to say something is larger, better, worse, etc. than it really is; to overstate
sabotage secret actions to destroy plans or property, or to interrupt activities
espionage spying; finding out political secrets and giving the information to the enemy
enforcement the carrying out of a rule or law
law-abiding respecting and obeying the law
disgrace shame; loss of honor and respect; public dishonor
mutual equally shared by each one (Here, each is equally suspicious of the other.)
coercive using force to make people do something they do not want to do
timid fearful; lacking courage

A. Vocabulary Check

Match the word with its definition.

____ 1. coercive	a. spying
____ 2. disgrace	b. relating to an action that forces someone to do something
____ 3. enforcement	c. sad; with little hope
____ 4. espionage	d. shame; loss of honor and respect
____ 5. exaggerate	e. to say something is better or worse than it really is
____ 6. gloomy	f. shy or fearful
____ 7. law-abiding	g. making sure a law is carried out
____ 8. mutual	h. shared equally by two people
____ 9. sabotage	i. obeying the laws
____ 10. timid	j. secret actions to destroy plans or property

B. Comprehension Check

Write the letter of the best answer according to the information in the chapter.

____ 1. In a televised address to the nation in July 1979 President Carter said that

a. the Vietnam war must be ended.
b. the future of America was very promising.
c. the American spirit was in decline.

____ 2. The majority of the American people were discouraged *mainly* by
a. the immorality of the Vietnam War.
b. failing to win the Vietnam War.
c. the amount of money wasted in the Vietnam War.

____ 3. Which of the following was *not* a part of the Watergate scandal?
a. The President accepted many bribes while he was in office.
b. Agents of the President conducted many illegal activities against his political opponents.
c. The President told the American people that he was innocent of all wrongdoing.

____ 4. In the 1970s and the 1980s Americans began to discover new limits on their material abundance in three important areas. Which of the following was *not* one of them?
a. water supplies
b. living space
c. farmland

____ 5. Public opinion experts observed that during the decade of the 1970s the American people
a. had developed a new sense of limits.
b. had an optimistic faith in the future.
c. had come to believe that most national problems could be solved.

____ 6. By the early 1980s public opinion experts observed that many Americans believed that
a. the present was the best time for their country.
b. the future would be the best time for their country.
c. the past was the best time for their country.

____ 7. President Ronald Reagan tends to believe that
a. business institutions do much more good for the nation's values than government institutions.
b. government institutions do much more good for the nation's values than business institutions.
c. business and government institutions are equally good for the nation's values.

____ 8. Conservation has never been a strong value in the United States *mainly* because
a. business has been a dominant institution.
b. the nation's resources have been vast.
c. political leaders have always discouraged it.

____ 9. Which of the following is *not* one of the values that works against a spirit of national cooperation in the United States?
a. individual freedom
b. competition
c. hard work

10. Which of the following aspects of its historical experience was given as an explanation of why the value of national cooperation is weak in the United States?
    a. Americans have never had to follow the directions of unelected leaders.
    b. Americans were permanently divided by the Civil War.
    c. Americans have never had their homeland invaded by a foreign enemy.

C. Questions for Discussion and Composition

1. What effect did the Vietnam War and Watergate have on the American people? How do people in your country view the American role in Vietnam? If a leader in your country did what President Nixon did, would he be forced out of office? What kind of government scandals have there been in your country?
2. What effect will the decline of material abundance have on the United States? What effect has the level of material abundance in your country had on the people and their values?
3. Do people in your country believe that the United States will continue to be strong or that America is declining? Is American influence declining in your country?
4. How would you compare your country's policies on conservation with those of the United States? Is conservation important in your country? Are there any serious shortages in your country? What plans does your country have to serve its energy needs of the future?
5. How does the government of your country encourage national cooperation? Does your government set national priorities for industrial development or agricultural production? How much control over the economy does your government have?
6. In general, what do you think about the American values presented in this book? What values do you think Americans should change? Are there any values in your country that you think should be changed? If you were the leader of your country, what would you do?
7. Are you basically optimistic about the future? Why or why not?

D. Cloze Summary Paragraph

This paragraph summarizes the chapter. Fill in each blank with any word that makes sense.

In the 1960s and ___*1970s*___ Americans faced three challenges ______________ their values. The loss ______________ the Vietnam War caused _______________ to question the strength _______________ their country and its _______________. The Watergate scandal weakened _______________ faith in the Presidency, _______________ the decline in material _______________ threatened to lower their _______________ of living. Faced with _______________ about the future, some _______________ to return to the _______________. Public opinion polls showed _______________ by 1980 many Americans _______________ that life was better _______________ the past than in _______________ present or the future. _______________ elected President in 1980, _______________ to return to the _______________ before 1930 when business _______________ strong and government was _______________. Other leaders believe instead _______________ Americans should develop new _______________ to go along with _______________ old values. There should _______________ a greater emphasis on _______________ of natural resources and _______________ national cooperation. The belief _______________ the freedom of the _______________ and the value of _______________ have discouraged national cooperation _______________ the past, but if _______________ is to meet the _______________ of the future, some _______________ in priorities will be _______________.

E. Outlining

Write an outline for this chapter. Remember to use the correct form and to avoid mixing sentence and topic entries. (See instructions for outlining exercises for Chapters 10 and 11.) Here is information about the organization of the chapter which may help you.

The first section deals with the challenge to American values—the Vietnam War, the Watergate scandal, and the decline of abundance. Which of these four should be the Roman numeral entry?

The challenge to American values
The Vietnam War
The Watergate scandal
The decline of abundance

Look for information to use as supporting details for each lettered entry. Be sure to watch for clues such as, "Three aspects of the affair [Watergate] made it the most serious scandal in American history." Use these three points as supporting details under "The Watergate scandal" entry.

The next section of the chapter, "A Return to the Past," is a transition from the first section to the third, "The Need for New National Values." This section is very short compared with the first and third sections. Should it be included as a main point (lettered entry) in the first or third section, or should it stand on its own as a separate section of the outline (Roman numeral entry)?

The third section deals with the need to develop two new values for the future. The first is conservation. What is the second? Skim the section to find the sentence that begins the discussion of the need for this second belief. Look for information to use as supporting details (numbers) for both values.

The last section, "What of the Future?" is also very short. Should it be included as a lettered entry in the previous section, or should it stand on its own (Roman numeral)?

F. Paraphrasing

Skim the chapter to find the three reasons why the Watergate scandal was the most serious in American history and paraphrase these reasons. State them in your own words. Find the passage dealing with the election of Ronald Reagan in 1980. Explain in your own words why his election in 1980 represented a desire by many Americans to return to the past.

G. Ask Americans

Find out what Americans think about the future. Ask the following questions and record Americans' answers. On the basis of your findings do you think Americans are basically optimistic or pessimistic about the future?

1. Do you think America's best days are behind it or in the future?
2. What do you think your chances of achieving "the good life" are?
   Very good
   Fairly good
   Not very good
   Not good at all

3. Thinking now of your parents when they were your age, would you say you are better off financially or not as well off financially as they were?
4. When you are older, do you expect to own more possessions than your parents do now, about the same, or less?
5. Do you agree or disagree with these statements:

   Young people can no longer take for granted that they will be able to live better than their parents.

   People like me don't have much of a chance to be successful in life.
6. Now, thinking of your children when they get to be your age, would you say they will be better off financially than you are now or not as well off?
7. Where do you think the truly important work in solving our country's problems will be done in the next ten years or so—the government or private organizations?
8. At the present time, do you think environmental protection laws and regulations have gone too far, not gone far enough, or struck about the right balance?
9. Which of these statements comes closer to your own feelings?

   We need to relax our environmental laws in order to achieve economic growth.

   or

   We need to maintain present environmental laws in order to preserve the environment for future generations.
10. There is still a controversy over energy needs and protecting the environment. Some people say that an adequate supply of energy is worth any risks to the environment. Others feel that it is better to risk not having enough energy than to risk spoiling the environment. Which side are you on? Are you more on the side of adequate energy or more on the side of protecting the environment?

H. Ask Yourself

Do you agree or disagree with these statements?

1. No country can win a nuclear war. — Agree Disagree
2. Nuclear power plants are basically safe and are good sources of energy for the future. — Agree Disagree
3. If all countries had nuclear weapons, the risk of nuclear war would be reduced. — Agree Disagree
4. Protecting the environment is more important than industrial development. — Agree Disagree
5. I expect to have more material possessions than my parents do now. — Agree Disagree
6. I am confident that my children will have as good a life as mine or better. — Agree Disagree

7. There is a good possibility that a nuclear war could destroy life on most of the earth. Agree Disagree
8. I would not want to be one of the survivors of a nuclear war. Agree Disagree
9. Science and technology do more to improve the overall quality of life than do religion and philosophy. Agree Disagree
10. I am basically optimistic about the future. Agree Disagree

I. Ask Americans

Below are listed some of the things people are concerned about today. Ask Americans to look at this list and choose the two or three things that they are *personally* most concerned about today.

Inflation and high prices
Crime and lawlessness
Money enough to live right and pay the bills
The fuel and energy crisis
The way the courts are run
A recession and rising unemployment
Our relations with foreign countries
Wrongdoing by elected government officials
Getting into another war
Drug abuse
The way young people think and act today
Pollution of air and water
Alcoholism

J. Suggestions for Writing

1. In February 1979 Charles Schultz, then chairman of the President's Council of Economic Advisors, said that "The pie is growing less rapidly, and both government and private demand are going to have to be scaled down accordingly." How does this statement relate to the picture of the future discussed in this chapter? What do you think will be the effect of this "smaller pie" (in terms of economic assets) on the public interest groups? On the lifestyle of individuals?
2. How much control do we as individuals have over the future? How much of our lives are in our own hands? Write an essay in which you take one of these three positions:
   The future of the world is in our hands
   We have little control over our destiny
   We may not be able to control the future, but we can shape it

3. In an article in *U.S. News and World Report* (July 5, 1982) entitled "America's Problem: 'Trying to Do Everything for Everybody,' " Theodore H. White, a well-known political analyst, discusses America's problems. He says that ever since the early 1960s Americans have been making promises—

> ...promises to save the cities, promises to take care of the sick, the old, the universities. By 1980 we had promised ourselves almost to the point of national bankruptcy .... Many of our problems flow out of American goodwill, trying to do everything for everybody .... In the 1960s we exploded with goodwill as blacks, who had been denied equality, rightfully demanded it. We could afford it, and we should have done what we did. But we have ended up pushing equality and other ideas to absurd limits as we sought perfect equality rather than realistic equality of opportunity .... We have to choose what we can do; we have to discipline our goodwill.*

How much can and should a nation do to ensure equality of opportunity for its people? Write a composition on the future of the value of equality of opportunity.

K. Write a Summary

The columnist Ellen Goodman wrote a newspaper column entitled "That Something Called Progress" after hearing the speech by President Carter mentioned at the beginning of this chapter. The following selection is the conclusion of that article. Read it carefully and write a summary of it.

> Carter criticized those who "worship self-indulgence and consumerism." Yet the notion of progress in America has been largely an individualistic and materialistic one: more for me.
>
> For the poor and the immigrant, "getting ahead" was an unequivocal desire for more. For most parents, it has meant raising children who achieved beyond them—more education, more success, more goods. And for the economy progress was measured in new improved things—washing machines, cars, disposals ....
>
> Only a few, like Lewis Mumford, observed about Americans: "They have confused progress with mechanization."
>
> Now, it seems that our faith in "something called progress" has been undermined in diverse and sometimes contradictory ways.
>
> We have lost faith in both its continuation and its value. The have-nots are afraid they'll never get the goodies, while the haves question the value of these goodies.

The have-less worry that their children won't have the opportunity to achieve beyond them. Yet, the privileged and the achieving see both the trade-offs they have made and the inevitable ceiling.

Carter's speech was really an attempt to shore up our confidence against slipping backward. But the fact is that we need a dialogue to define a new kind of progress.

Inside the circumference of our fear of the future is a profound skepticism about the present. We are afraid of seeing the end of a "progressive era." And yet we no longer are convinced that progress is progress anymore.*

L. Suggestions for Further Reading

Robert Woodward and Carl Bernstein. *All the President's Men.*
Alvin Toffler. *The Third Wave.*
Alvin Toffler. *Future Shock.*
George Orwell. *1984.*
Aldous Huxley. *Brave New World.*
Theodore Roszak. *The Making of a Counter Culture.*

New Word Index

The number after each word indicates the chapter in which the word was first introduced.

University of Texas at Austin News and Information Service, Duquesne University Tamburitzans, Sirovich Senior Center, Joseph Keyerleber, Ken Karp, Larry Murphy, Irene Springer, Diane Stanford.
Collage design by Frances M. Kasturas.

PARIS
FDNY
K879
THE UNIVERSITY OF TEXAS
Longhorn Band
The Show Band of the Southwest